*f*P

The Customer Marketing Method

How to implement and profit
from customer relationship management

Jay Curry
with Adam Curry

THE FREE PRESS

New York London Toronto Sydney Singapore

THE FREE PRESS
A Division of Simon & Schuster, Inc.
1230 Avenue of the Americas
New York, NY 10020

Designed by MM Design 2000, Inc.

Manufactured in the United States of America

10 9 8 7 6 5 4 3 2 1

Library of Congress Cataloging-in-Publication Data

Curry, Jay
    The customer marketing method : how to implement and profit from customer
relationship management / Jay Curry with Adam Curry.
        p. cm.
    1. Customer relations—Management. 2. Consumers' preferences. 3. Relationship
marketing. I. Curry, Adam. II. Title

    HF5415.5 .C828 2000
    658.8'12—dc21   99-089747

ISBN 0–684–83943–1

Contents

Thanksgiving

This book would not have been possible without the support and involvement of:

- My clients—customers—who keep teaching me every day what customer relationship management is all about.
- My son Adam, whose contribution can be found in Part Three.
- My business partners—Wil Wurtz, Conny Zijlstra, and Guido Thys—who added a whole lot of value and structure to convert a concept into a method.
- My life partners—Yolanda and Timothy—who endured the long hours when their husband/father sat for hours in front of the monitor in search of the right words.

Thanks.
Jay Curry

Frequently Asked Questions
About This Book

What is Customer Relationship Management?

Customer Relationship Management—or CRM—is an old subject that has become a hot topic.

Since the 1960s management gurus such as Peter Drucker and Theodore Levitt have been preaching the CRM gospel, which can be simply summarized like this:

> "The true business of every company is to make customers, keep customers, and maximize customer profitability."

This gospel was neglected by most companies—until recently. Why? Because only now are new and improved technologies (databases, datamining, Internet, etc.) capable of tracking and managing customer profitability, behavior, and satisfaction at a reasonable cost.

As a result, 70% of large companies expect to implement Customer Relationship Management in some form during the next five years, according to a recent study published by the *Economist* Intelligence Unit and Andersen Consulting.

What is Customer Marketing?

Customer Marketing® is a structured method that has been used by hundreds of companies to implement one or more aspects of CRM. The European Economic Community has supported the development of the Customer Marketing method and tools to improve the competitive position of European companies. This book introduces the method to American companies and managers.

What will I learn from this book?

This book is divided into three parts:

- Part One explains what CRM and Customer Marketing are and how they can lead to dramatic profit increases in your company.
- Part Two takes you through a step-by-step process to implement CRM in your company using the Customer Marketing method. The "InterTech" case is used to illustrate the steps. (You can read through it quickly the first time, then use it as a "cookbook" during your implementation project.)
- Part Three discusses how you can take advantage of the Internet to build better relationships with your customers—and to defend yourself against competitors who are trying to use the Internet to take your customers away from you.

What kinds of companies will profit most from this book: small, medium or large?

Implementing CRM with Customer Marketing is similar to implementation of a Total Quality Management program. It brings with it the need to change the activities and attitudes of managers and employees. It doesn't happen overnight.

Customer Marketing implementation works best at the level of Customer Teams—groups of sales, marketing, and service people, all of whom work with the same group of customers. Once you find out the right way to do this with a "pilot project," you can roll out the process throughout the company, no matter how large it is.

In short, the book is primarily written for

- Owners and CEOs of small to medium-size companies, up to around five hundred employees.
- Managers of business units in large companies who can operate relatively autonomously and/or have been selected to implement CRM as a pilot project.
- Large companies that want to improve the performance of their franchisees, distributors, dealers, and agents.

Where can I get additional information and guidance about Customer Marketing—without hiring a consultant?

The readers of this book are invited to visit *www.customermarketing.com,* where you will find out about more tools and information to help you implement CRM in your company.

Is this book for business-to-business or business-to-consumer companies?

CRM and Customer Marketing can work for any business—provided that it can capture and store customer names, sales revenues, and characteristics in some kind of software, the minimum being a simple spreadsheet.

And the authors draw on their experiences with companies selling to other businesses and to individual consumers.

The "InterTech" implementation case in Part Two of this book is a business-to-business example, since it demonstrates how CRM can be implemented in companies that employ a sales force in addition to other methods and media.

Is this book a value-for-money proposition?

The time and money you invest in this book can be quickly paid back many times by following up on only one of the many tips and suggestions you will find in it.

But you can get a huge return on investment from this book if

- You want to know how to increase the profitability, sales revenues, and satisfaction of the customers you now have.
- You want to know how to get some new customers, which will improve your bottom line results.
- You use the knowledge in this book to make it happen.

Part One

How to Profit from Customer Relationship Management With Customer Marketing

Chapter 1

"What Business Are You In?"

Has a consultant ever asked you this simple but profound question?

If so, he may have been trying to appear wise and all-knowing.

But more likely he was trying to see if you are *product oriented* or *market oriented.*

If you answer the question "What business are you in?" in relation to your primary product or service with, for example,

"We sell shoes."
"We are accountants."
"We build houses."

then you probably are rather product oriented. And this can be dangerous.

As Theodore Levitt pointed out in "Marketing Myopia," his classic *Harvard Business Review* article published in 1960, the presidents of American railway companies in the early 1900s, if asked, would have answered the question like this:

"We are in the business of operating trains."

The result of this narrow, product-oriented thinking was that virtually every U.S. rail company went bankrupt or faced serious problems because they missed out on the rapid growth of the airlines and the development of a sophisticated highway system as a way to get things and people from place A to place B.

For the railroads, a better answer would have been

"We are in the transportation business."

Another example is IBM. Thomas Watson, Jr., son of the IBM founder, tells in his book, *Father, Son & Co.,* how IBM almost missed out on the computer revolution in the early 1950s. Many IBM-ers—including his forceful father—would have answered the question this way:

"We are in the business of supplying punch card machinery."

The old-guard IBM-ers were making huge profits selling the machines that processed the cards carrying the famous "Do not fold, spindle, or mutilate" admonition. They simply refused to believe in the benefits of magnetic tape as a medium to store data and in computers to process that data. Watson Jr., hearing major customers such as Time, Inc. complain about the costs of storing and managing millions of punch cards, realized just in time that IBM's answer to the question should be

"We are in the business of data processing."

By exploiting and developing computer technology as a better, faster, and cheaper way to process data, IBM became one of the largest and most successful companies in the world. (They have had ups and downs since then, but at the end of the day, IBM listens to their customers. That's why they are a leader in e-commerce today.)

As these examples indicate, a market orientation is much healthier for you and your business in this fast-changing world.

But now the politically correct answer is

"We are in business to make customers, keep customers, and maximize customer profitability."

Business owners and managers have rediscovered the customer. And so should you—if you haven't already.

Your company's revenues, profits, and market share—and your salary—come ultimately from only one source: *your customers!*

No matter what product or service you provide—be it candy bars, computers, insurance, or temporary help—customers are the heart of your business. When you get right down to it, the one single thing a company needs to be in business is a customer!

- You don't need money to be in business.
- You don't need to have an idea to be in business.
- You don't need a store, factory, or office location to be in business.
- You don't need personnel to be in business.
- You don't even need a product or service to be in business.

All these things help, of course. But without a customer, you're not in business.

If you have just one customer, you are in business.

If you have a lot of *good customers,* you have a successful business.

If your company is successful—and I hope it is—I'm willing to bet you have developed a solid base of good customers who do nice things like this:

- *Buy more from you—even if your prices are (somewhat) higher than the competition's.*
  Obviously, you can't gouge people and expect to get away with it. But think about that small grocery store or specialty clothing store where they know your name or the service is pleasant. Sure, you pay a bit more. But you keep coming back.
- *Recommend you to colleagues, family, friends.*
  There's no better promotional message than a recommendation from a satisfied customer. People talk about their experiences with suppliers—both good and bad. A recent study showed that Information Technology managers rate advice from colleagues as one of the most important sources of information for buying a system— and that more than 60% of IT managers give advice privately to colleagues outside their own organization!
  Imagine—the IT manager of Proctor & Gamble meets the IT manager of Unilever at a computer conference. They don't talk about soap. They talk about who's doing what to whom in the IT community—and their experiences, good and bad, with suppliers.
  While a good customer will generate a lot of business for you, a dissatisfied customer can hurt you badly. Who was it who said:

"For every complaint there are 10 others who didn't make the effort to tell you of their dissatisfaction. And since every dissatisfied customer gripes to an average of 6 people, every complaint represents 60 people who are walking around with a negative image of your company."

- *Make you the "standard" for the organization or family.*
  What could be better than having the boss at your customer site send out a memo to all employees: "All [name of your product or service] must be ordered from [name of your company]"! Good customers write memos like that.

- *Try out your new products and help you make them better.*
  Good customers are usually willing to invest their time and effort to help you develop and improve your (new) products and services. In the case of software and sophisticated technology, customer involvement in research and development of new products can be worth millions of dollars or more in man-hours and expertise. And the beauty part is this: *As customers become involved in your business, they tend to become better customers!*

- *Use your support, service, and other facilities.*
  Service, support, training, add-ons. These often highly profitable products and services are usually offered to customers with whom you have a good relationship.

Do you believe that getting, keeping, and maximizing the profitability of good customers is so essential for the continuity of your business?

Then you will probably want to know how customer pyramids can help you understand and manage your customers better than you now do.

Read all about them in the next chapter.

Chapter 2

All About Customer Pyramids

A customer pyramid is a useful tool to help you visualize, analyze, and improve the behavior and profitability of your customers.

You can also use a customer pyramid to create more customer awareness among managers and staff in your company. Replace the sterile monthly sales charts on the company cafeteria walls with customer pyramids that graphically illustrate what is really happening in the real world each month: the up-down/in-out behavior of your customers.

Figure 2.1

Basic Elements of a Customer Pyramid

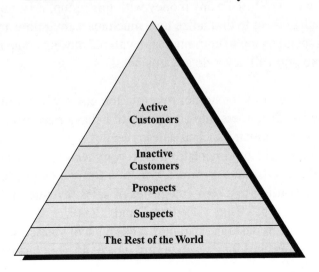

The following are the basic elements of a customer pyramid (see Figure 2.1):

- *Active Customers*—persons or companies that have purchased goods or services from your company within a given period, say, the last 12 months.
- *Inactive Customers*—persons or companies that have purchased goods or services from your company in the past but not within the given period. Inactive customers are an important source of potential revenue—and also a source of information about what you need to do to prevent your Active Customers from becoming Inactive Customers!
- *Prospects*—persons or companies with whom you have some kind of relationship—but they have not yet purchased any goods or services. Examples of Prospects are people who have responded to a mailing and requested your brochure; companies that have issued you a request for bid; contacts met at a trade fair. The Prospects, of course, are persons and companies you expect to upgrade to Active Customer status in the near future.
- *Suspects*—persons or companies that you could be able to serve with your products and services—but you do not yet have a relationship with them. Normally, you seek to begin a relationship with Suspects and qualify them as Prospects, with the longer-term goal of converting them to Active Customers.
- *The Rest of the World*—persons or companies that simply have no need or desire to purchase or use your products and services. While you will never make any money with this group, it is important to visualize them to dramatize how much marketing time and money you spend trying to communicate with people and companies with whom you will never do any business!

The value of the customer pyramid increases when you segment your Active Customers into categories of behavior critical to the success of your company, such as sales revenue.

After a lot of experimentation, we recommend for most companies a "standard" customer pyramid, which is formed by clustering customers according to a four categories of sales revenues as shown in Figure 2.2: "Top," "Big," "Medium," and "Small."

To create this customer pyramid, make a list of your customers with their sales revenues for a given period (normally, your last fiscal year).

Figure 2.2

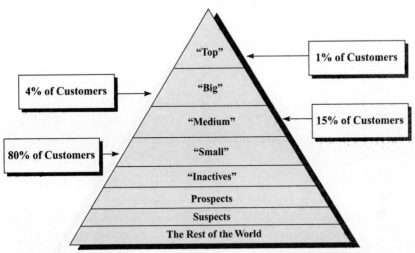

**Standard Customer Pyramid
(based on sales revenues)**

This information should be available in your bookkeeping department.

You then sort the customer list from top to bottom, beginning with the largest customer in terms of sales and ending with the smallest customer. (A spreadsheet program such as Excel or Lotus 1-2-3 makes this task more manageable.) What you end up with is what we call a "customer sort."

You then segment the list of customers into four categories, as follows:

- *"Top" Customers*—the top 1% of your active customers in terms of sales revenue. (If you have 1,000 active customers, your "Top" Customers would be the first 10 customers on your list.)
- *"Big" Customers*—the next 4% of your active customers in terms of sales revenue. (If you have 1,000 active customers, your "Big" Customers would be the next 40 customers on your list.)
- *"Medium" Customers*—the next 15% of your active customers in terms of sales revenue. (If you have 1,000 active customers, your "Medium" Customers would be the next 150 customers on your list.)
- *"Small" Customers*—the remaining 80% of your active customers in terms of sales revenue. (If you have 1,000 active customers,

Figure 2.3

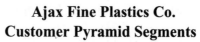

Ajax Fine Plastics Co.
Customer Pyramid Segments

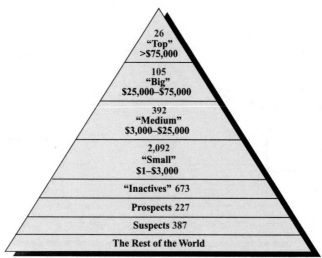

your "Small" Customers would be the remaining 800 customers on your list.)

To complete your customer pyramid, add the number of "Inactives" (Inactive Customers) (they can also be found in your bookkeeping records), your active Prospects (ask the sales department), and your Suspects (ask the marketing department). For the moment, don't worry yet about the Rest of the World.

Figure 2.3 shows an example of a customer pyramid for the "Ajax Fine Plastics Co.," which has 2,615 active customers. Thus Ajax had 26 "Top," 105 "Big," 392 "Medium," and 2,092 "Small" Customers.

Notice also the customer pyramid segment "boundaries," which will become evident from your customer sort.

For Ajax, a "Top" Customer spends more than $75,000; a "Big" Customer spends between $25,000 and $75,000; a "Medium" Customer spends between $3,000 and $25,000; and "Small" Customers spend from $1 to $3,000. (Note: We will come back to the Ajax Fine Plastics shortly.)

Some companies and industries find it more practical or useful

Figure 2.4

Banking/Insurance Customer Pyramid
(based on number of products per customer)

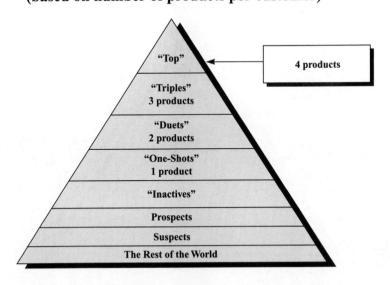

to work with a customer pyramid based on behavior other than sales revenues.

For instance, the financial industry (banks and insurance) can segment customers based on the number of products or product clusters purchased or used by each customer. For instance, the "One Shots"—often 80% or more of a bank or insurance company's customers—have only one account or insurance policy; "Duets" have two; "Triples," three; and so on (See Figure 2.4).

For many retail organizations, the number of visits per customer is a key—and measurable—factor. For food stores, the number of visits per month is important. For clothing stores (and hairdressers!), the number of visits per year are used to build a customer pyramid (see Figure 2.5).

Companies that sell capital goods, such as machines, trucks, and automobiles, may prefer to work with a customer pyramid based on the number of consecutive purchases made by a customer over a long period of time (see Figure 2.6). For instance, an auto dealer would count a customer who has purchased four or more automobiles in the past as a "Top" customer; the customer who has purchased three as a "Triple"; and so on.

Figure 2.5

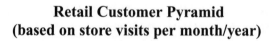

Retail Customer Pyramid
(based on store visits per month/year)

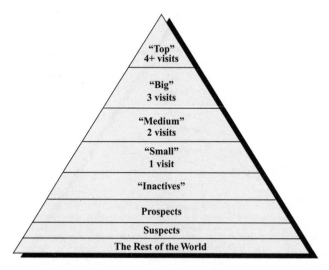

By the way, since many capital goods suppliers also sell services and "consumables," they often find that a customer pyramid based on yearly gross margin (sales revenues less costs of goods and services) is even more useful.

Customer Pyramids for Each Company Level

Customer pyramids can be built to reflect the hierarchical structure and size of your company. A small company may have only one pyramid for all customers. Larger companies can have a customer pyramid at the corporate, regional, and on down to the sales territory level (see Figure 2.7).

It is essential, however, that the customer pyramids maintain the same customer definitions and that the structure remain the same for all levels. This allows for customer reporting up and down the line—how many customers were gained, lost, upgraded, downgraded, etc. It adds a new dimension to the typical financial reporting.

For instance, one Swiss company established a pyramid for scores of sales offices around the world with these parameters in Swiss francs:

Figure 2.6

Capital Goods Customer Pyramid
(based on number of consecutive purchases)

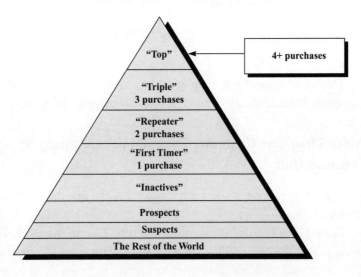

Figure 2.7

Multi-Level Customer Pyramids

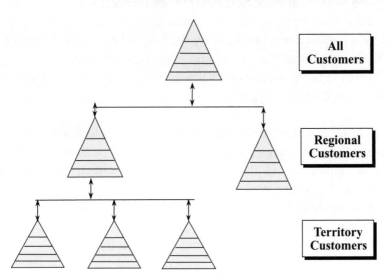

Top Customer: >100,000

Large Customer: 50,000–100,000

Medium Customer: 25,000–50,000

Small Customer: 1–25,000

This system gave top management a clear view of their worldwide customer base, translated into the one currency of relevance.

More Than One Customer Pyramid per Company or Business Unit

Most managers have no problem answering the question "Who is your customer?"

The retailer knows his customer who comes into the store. The temporary help agency counts the personnel department as its customer. The insurance brokers sell either to private individuals or a corporate decision-making unit.

But sometimes defining the customer is not so simple. For instance, if you are a food processor with branded products, who is the customer? The distributor that buys the product directly from you? The supermarket that buys from the distributor? Or the individual shopper who buys from the supermarket? (See Figure 2.8.)

And who is the customer for a producer of prescription drugs? The doctor who prescribes the drug? Or the hospital that buys the drug directly from the producer or the wholesaler? (See Figure 2.9.)

There are two guidelines for helping you define your customers and define your customer pyramids.

1. *Make pyramids for those customers whose behavior you can influence.* It doesn't make sense to spend a lot of time tracking companies or individuals in the "food chain" over which you have no influence. Therefore, a prescription drug company may have a customer pyramid only for the prescribing doctor who is visited by the "detail man." But a food processor may have customer pyramids for the distributor, the supermarkets, and individual households.

Figure 2.8

Customer Pyramids: Distribution Channels

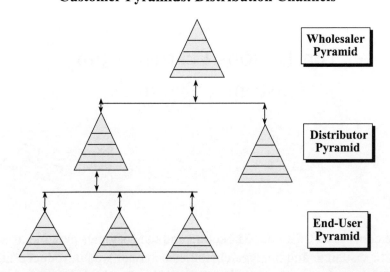

2. *Make pyramids for customers requiring different marketing and sales methods.* You may have a product that you sell to end users and to distributors or dealers. If you have split your sales force into direct and indirect business units, you may find it useful to make completely different pyramids for each business unit in order to make performance comparisons and to allow for differences in customer (contact) plans.

Figure 2.9

Some companies have more than one customer pyramid

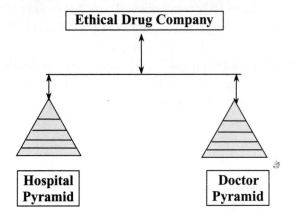

Chapter 3

Ten Lessons Learned from Customer Pyramids

The concept of Customer Marketing and the customer pyramid as a tool to visualize and analyze customer behavior was introduced in 1989. Since then we have built and looked at hundreds of customer pyramids for companies in a wide variety of industries. Electronic component manufacturers . . . wholesalers . . . automobile dealers . . . retailers . . . manufacturers of fast-moving consumer goods . . . banks and insurers . . . even law firms!

While these companies have been wildly different in terms of size and types of business, their customer pyramids reflect remarkably similar patterns of customer behavior. And the ways in which all these companies interact with their customers are also remarkably similar.

From our experiences with these companies, we have been able to distill and share with you 10 lessons learned from customer pyramids.

To illustrate these 10 lessons, we will use "Ajax Fine Plastics Co." (AFP) as a case. (Finally, I can follow the advice given to Dustin Hoffman in *The Graduate* and . . . get into plastics!)

While Ajax is a fictional name of a fictional company, the customer pyramids are very real and are quite representative of the situation in the business-to-business marketplace.

Just to set the background, here is some basic data on Ajax Fine Plastics:

- 2,615 customers
- $13,669,000 annual revenues
- $588,654 operational profit

Figure 3.1

Customer Pyramid of Ajax Fine Plastics Co.

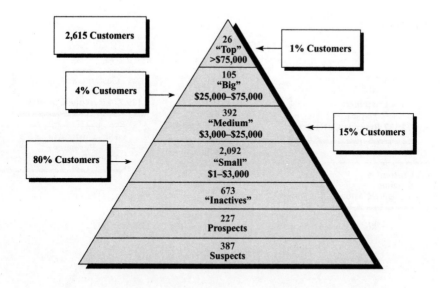

- $5,227 revenue per customer
- $225 operational profit per customer

Figure 3.1 shows the AFP customer pyramid.

You will probably want to compare your own customer pyramid and activities to see which—if any—of the 10 lessons apply to your situation.

Lesson 1

The top 20% of the customers deliver 80% of revenues.

Just about every customer pyramid we have ever constructed or seen proves the validity of the 80/20 Pareto Principle. There are, of course, some variances, from 70/30 to 90/10. But the revenue analysis is almost always in the 80/20 ballpark.

The revenue distribution of AFP is also quite normal; that is, revenue contribution per customer segment does not vary greatly. There are exceptions: some business-to-business companies derive a great deal of revenues from a very small number of customers. The customer pyramid will reveal this vulnerability.

We once presented a customer pyramid to 500 employees of an IT

Figure 3.2

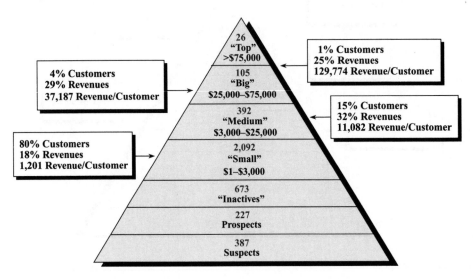

1% Customers
25% Revenues
129,774 Revenue/Customer

4% Customers
29% Revenues
37,187 Revenue/Customer

15% Customers
32% Revenues
11,082 Revenue/Customer

80% Customers
18% Revenues
1,201 Revenue/Customer

26
"Top"
>$75,000

105
"Big"
$25,000–$75,000

392
"Medium"
$3,000–$25,000

2,092
"Small"
$1–$3,000

673
"Inactives"

227
Prospects

387
Suspects

company that showed that 1 % of their customers—16 in number—were good for 49% of revenue. The customer pyramid demonstrated with facts and figures that the departure of just one of these customers could mean bankruptcy. (The "customer care" attitudes of these employees improved quite quickly as a result of the presentation.)

Lesson 2

The top 20% of the customers deliver more than 100% of profits.

Now you can understand why all airline companies have "frequent flyer" programs—a relatively small percentage of their passengers deliver all the profits, and more.

Put another way, the airlines—like most companies—lose money on 80% of their customers!

If you fairly allocate all costs—product, overheads, and marketing/sales—spent on each customer or customer segment in the customer pyramid, you will probably discover this amazing fact of business life holds true for you as well.

Figure 3.3

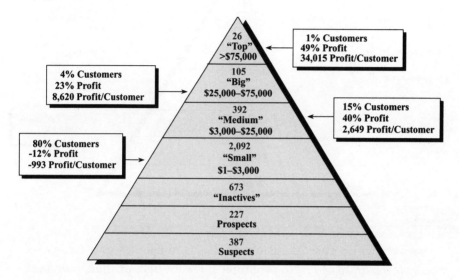

Take, for instance, the average revenue of your small customers. Then deduct the cost of product or services to arrive at the gross margin per small customer. If you then deduct the cost per company for invoicing, customer service, and one or two sales visits at $150 each, then there is not much contribution—if any—left over for the shareholders.

With the AFP example, small customers deliver an average of $1,201 in revenues. The cost of invoicing and collecting the revenues— plus a sales visit or two—eats up the margin for these customers.

(Later on in this book we will discuss how "Customer-Based Accounting" techniques can help you measure the profitability of the customers in your pyramid.)

Lesson 3

Existing customers deliver up to 90% of revenues.

This is a profound lesson to be learned from customer pyramids because it drives home the fact of life that companies can stay in busi-

Figure 3.4

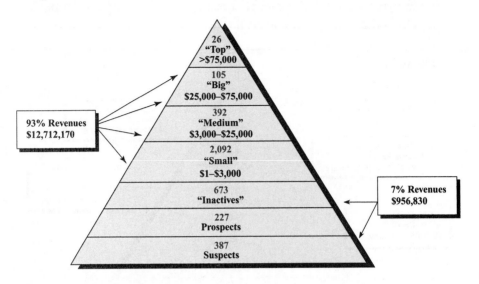

ness only with a base of customers. Even companies only two years old, we have discovered, often get 60% to 70% of their revenues from existing customers. And yet most managers I talk to are not conscious of the fact that 90% of their business comes from current customers.

I was once challenged at a seminar by an executive whose business was moving industrial plants from one country to another. He said that his service was a once-in-a-lifetime deal for his customers—he had virtually no customers that moved a plant more than once and thus had no repeat business. But, upon questioning, he revealed that his real "customers" were a handful of engineers who managed plant relocation projects. These engineers were good for about 80% of his revenues.

Lesson 4

The bulk of marketing budgets is often spent on noncustomers.

Although every company gets about 90% of their revenue from existing customers, most companies spend much (60% to 80%) of their marketing money communicating with noncustomers.

Figure 3.5

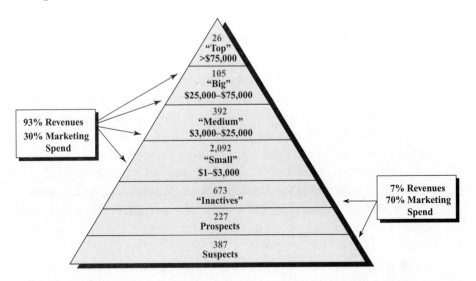

Of course it takes much more time, effort, and money to make a sale to a noncustomer than to a customer. Why? Because a sale to a noncustomer means the creation of a customer. And customer creation often requires a lot of persuasion, not just to sell the product or service but to overcome the doubts and fears that prospects and suspects have when considering whether or not to spend money with a new supplier.

The problem is that a great deal of the marketing budget spent on noncustomers is often wasted on "The Rest of the World." Take diapers for example. TV advertisements for diapers run during prime time are seen in 100% of all households watching television. But of these households, only 8% have diaper-age children. Thus there is a guaranteed waste of 92% of the television budget, which is targeted at "The Rest of the World."

The focus on noncustomers also has a psychological element. Marketing and sales people often get a bigger kick from getting "new business" than from taking a routine order from an old, familiar, and faithful customer.

But we will see why more attention paid to some existing customers can deliver a dramatic growth in profits.

Lesson 5

Between 5% and 30% of all customers have the potential for upgrading in the customer pyramid.

While most companies lose money on their "Small" Customers, this should not lead to a wholesale purge, such as sending them off to the competition or turning them over to dealers and distributors. One reason is that the 20% of revenues from "Small" Customers provides a contribution to overheads and helps build economies of scale.

More important, a number of "Small" Customers have the potential to move quickly to the top of the pyramid. Not necessarily because their needs for your products and services will increase dramatically, but because your "share of customer" is low. In other words, the "Small" Customer in your pyramid may be a "Top" Customer in the pyramid of your competitor!

The marketing manager of a computer company once confessed to me that he wanted to get rid of all customers who spent less than $5,000 each year. But he changed his mind when, making his customer pyramid, he discovered that one of his "Small" Customers for the past two years was KLM, the airline company, which was currently spending tens of millions of dollars per year on computer hardware, software, and services.

And it is not just "Small" Customers that can be upgraded. A num-

Figure 3.6

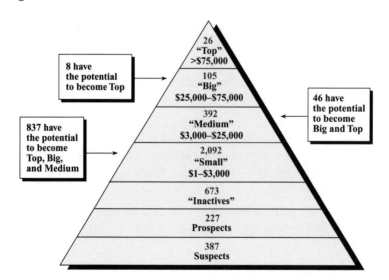

ber of your "Medium" and "Big" Customers may have a need for additional products and services that you offer—but you haven't yet bothered to do any cross-selling.

But customer upgrading also has a lot to do with customer satisfaction.

Lesson 6

Customer satisfaction is critical for migration up the pyramid.

We have done some studies on the relationship between customer satisfaction and customer behavior. And without fail, there is a strong correlation between upward migration in the customer pyramid and customer satisfaction.

But the most comprehensive and most recent research on this topic was done by Jones and Sasser, published in the article "Why Satisfied Customers Defect" in the December 1995 issue of the *Harvard Business Review.*

This study reveals how much customer satisfaction really pays off at the bottom line.

For instance, the *highly* satisfied Xerox customers had a repeat sales rate *six times higher* than that of customers who said that they were just plain "satisfied."

Figure 3.7

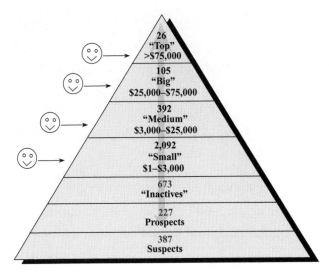

In today's competitive environment with high production and service standards, people expect *all* their suppliers to perform at a satisfactory level.

So if your customers tell you they are "satisfied," watch out!

Lesson 7

Reasonably satisfied customers often defect to the competition.

Figure 3.8

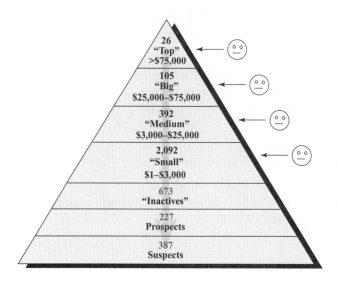

Lesson 8

Marketing and sales are responsible for influencing customer behavior.

If you ask marketing and sales people what they do for a living, you will get answers like: "We identify and satisfy needs" . . . "We sell products and services" . . . "We develop and maintain relationships."

But at the end of the day, marketing and sales departments people have the task to *influence the behavior of (potential) customers.*

Marketing and sales people are charged with the heavy responsibility of:

Figure 3.9

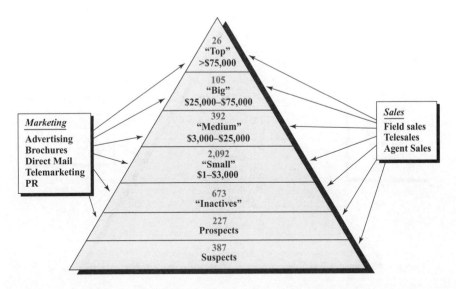

- Identifying (qualified) prospects from a pool of suspects, eliminating from consideration, when possible, "The Rest of the World."
- Creating new customers.
- Reactivating inactive customers.
- Keeping those customers who have reached the top of their spending levels.
- Upgrading customers where the company's "share of customer" can be improved.

But marketing and sales are not the only departments and people involved with customers.

Lesson 9

Other departments and people also influence customer behavior—for better or worse.

Other departments and people in your company have a great deal of influence on customers, which may exceed that of marketing and sales!

Your marketing communications manager, for instance, may send

Figure 3.10

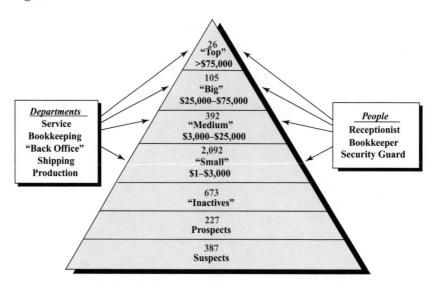

Departments	26 "Top" >$75,000
Service	105 "Big" $25,000–$75,000
Bookkeeping	392 "Medium" $3,000–$25,000
"Back Office"	2,092 "Small" $1–$3,000
Shipping	
Production	

out four mailings per year to customers. But another department—accounts receivable—sends those same customers a minimum of twelve very important mailings each year: the invoices! And if the invoices are incorrect or hard to understand, the influence on the customer may be quite negative at that critical moment in the relationship when money must be transferred to your company.

And let's say you have a new and inexperienced account manager who visits his accounts six times a year to build the relationship (and sell some product). Potential customer dissatisfaction caused by his lack of experience may be more than compensated for by a savvy service technician who keeps the customer happy with extra service and "stroking" when he also shows up six times a year for maintenance calls.

In short, the task of influencing customer behavior is the task of everyone in the organization.

But if you accept this premise, you need to ask yourself some critical questions about "non-marketing/sales" managers and employees:

- Do they understand the importance of customers to the health and continuity of the company?
- Are they aware of their role in identifying, creating, keeping, and upgrading customers?

- Do they have the experience and know-how to play that role successfully?
- Have they access to the customer information they need?

Lesson 10

A 2% upward migration in the customer pyramid can mean 10% more revenues and 50% more profit!

This is the real profit payoff of Customer Relationship Management!

Some of your Active Customers will depart, die, or disappear every year. Some Prospects and Suspects will become new customers. Some customers will drop down in the pyramid during the year; others will move up.

But if you can manage your customers to create a net upward migration in your customer pyramid, you, your boss, and your shareholders will be very happy!

As the AFP case in Figure 3.11 shows, a net upward migration of 17 customers (0.65%) in the customer pyramid can deliver a 10% revenue increase and a whopping 61% jump in operational profit!

Figure 3.11

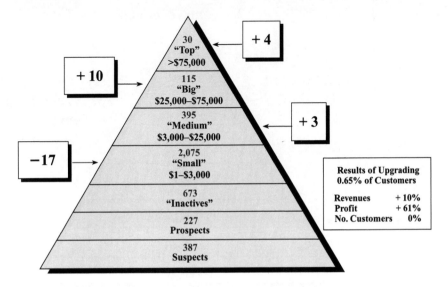

30 "Top" >$75,000	+ 4
115 "Big" $25,000–$75,000	+ 10
395 "Medium" $3,000–$25,000	+ 3
2,075 "Small" $1–$3,000	−17
673 "Inactives"	
227 Prospects	
387 Suspects	

Results of Upgrading 0.65% of Customers

Revenues	+ 10%
Profit	+ 61%
No. Customers	0%

Chapter 4

The Customer Marketing Strategy

The customer pyramids teach us that if you want to gain riches, power, and fame in the business world, you need only to follow this simple three-step Customer Marketing strategy.

1. Get new customers into your pyramid.
2. Move customers higher in your pyramid.
3. Keep customers from leaving the pyramid.

Figure 4.1

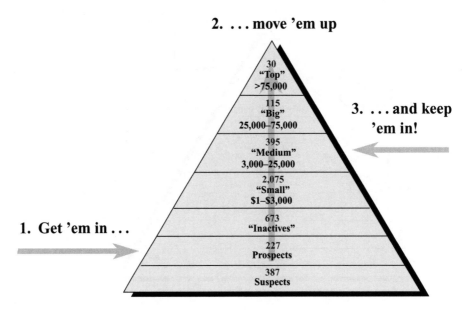

28

It's really quite simple.

But how can you best manage the relationship with your customers to make it happen?

That's what this book is all about.

Chapter 5

A Customer Relationship Management Model

After years of helping companies move customers up the pyramid, we have concluded that there are two kinds of customer-related success factors that can be measured and managed:

- Customer Performance Factors
- Customer Focus Factors

Let's look at these in more detail.

Customer Performance Factors

Customer Value

Operational profit is the result of deducting from the profit generated from profitable customers the losses generated from unprofitable customers. It's as simple as that.

Customer value is not derived from the gross profit or the margin of a customer (revenues less cost of products and services).

Marketing costs, sales costs, and overheads must also be deducted from margins.

For instance, you may make money on a small or medium-size customer who phones in repeat orders on a regular basis. But if you allow a salesperson to visit this customer six times a year because he is at-

Figure 5.1

Customer Performance Factors

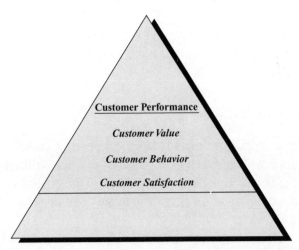

tracted to the front desk receptionist, the value of that customer is likely to become negative.

Customer Behavior

While cost factors play an important role in the profitability of a customer, customer value is to a large extent determined by *customer behavior.*

Customer behavior is usually measured in terms of *revenue*—either monetary or volume of product or services ordered over a period of time.

Positive customer behavior means, in the first place, that a *customer is a customer*—he buys from you in the first place.

A second customer behavior parameter is *customer lifetime,* or the average length of time, measured in months or years, that the average customer does business with you.

A third and important customer behavior factor is *"customer share":* the extent to which a customer meets his needs for the kinds of products or services he wants by doing business with you.

To illustrate customer share, let's use as an example an automobile dealer, Auto Smith.

Rapid Taxi has 20 vehicles, 18 of which were bought from Auto Smith, giving Smith a 90% share of customer Rapid Taxi.

Mega Couriers also bought 18 vehicles from Auto Smith—but these are only a fraction of his 200 vehicle fleet, giving Auto Smith only a 9% share of customer Mega Couriers. The customer behavior of Rapid Taxi is, of course, much more positive for Auto Smith than Mega Couriers.

Customer Satisfaction

Happy and satisfied customers behave in a positive manner. They will buy a lot from you and will give you a large share of their business. Customer satisfaction is derived largely from the quality and reliability of your products and services. You make good on your explicit and implied promises.

But as we have learned, customers who are only just satisfied are likely to walk away for a slightly more attractive proposition from your competitor. The major goal of customer satisfaction program should be to achieve "preferred supplier" status with as many customers as possible.

"Preferred supplier" status means that a customer formally or implicitly makes the policy known within the organization that whenever possible, any purchases of goods and services in your category will be supplied by . . . you!

The Customer Focus Factors

Customer Performance—customer value, customer behavior, and customer satisfaction—is something that happens *outside the company.* But Customer Performance is to a large extent determined by Customer Focus Factors *inside the company* and has a major impact on Customer Performance.

There are three primary and six secondary Customer Focus Factors:

A. Organization

1. Management is committed to Customer Focus, sets an example itself, and budgets time and money for customer process improvement.

Figure 5.2

Customer Focus Factors

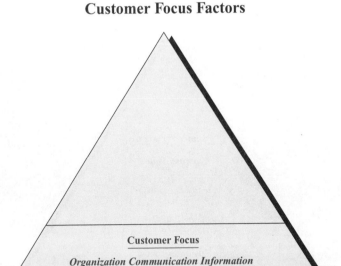

Customer Focus

Organization Communication Information

2. *Employees* possess the necessary customer care skills and experience, have a customer care attitude, and work in teams with others who have customer contacts.

B. Communications

3. *Contact logistics:* Customer communications are well planned, on time, with no sloppiness in execution.

4. The most appropriate *methods/media/messages* are applied to each customer (segment); communications are interactive, stress customer benefits rather than product features.

C. Information

5. Customer *data* is relevant, complete, and up-to-date.

6. Customer *information systems* are effective, flexible, and user-friendly.

There is clearly a direct correlation between Customer Focus and Customer Performance.

If you can improve your Customer Focus, you will improve Customer Performance (see Figure 5.3).

Figure 5.3

Customer Focus Influences Customer Performance

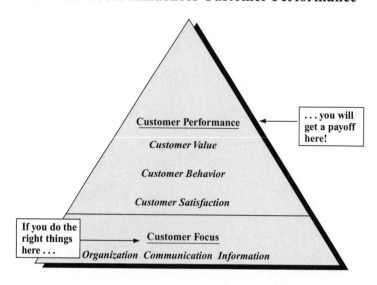

Putting Customer Performance and Customer Focus together brings us to a Customer Relationship Management model, as shown in Figure 5.4.

The model represents the idea that if your internal Customer Focus is strong, your customers will be very satisfied.

And if your customers are very satisfied, they will behave very nicely, giving you a large part of their business, often without any major marketing and sales effort or squeezing every cent off the price. ("Send me another thousand Widgets and the invoice.")

This positive customer behavior will lead to higher customer value—and therefore more operational profit!

It's quite a simple concept.

But . . . if you can't measure the factors in the Customer Relationship Management model, you can't manage them (see Figure 5.5).

There is a whole tribe of professionals out there measuring your profits—the accountants.

But is anyone measuring customer profitability, customer behavior, customer satisfaction, and customer focus so that they can be managed and improved?

Figure 5.4

A Customer Relationship Management Model

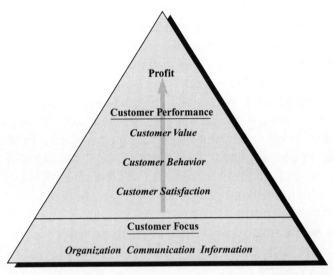

Figure 5.5

"If you can't measure it, you can't manage it."

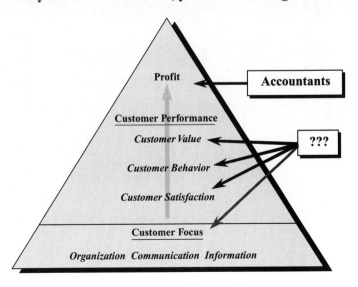

The answer all too often is this: not really.

If you ask a sales manager who his ten largest customers are, he may be able to name some or even all of them. But you will search for a long time to find someone who can tell you within 24 hours the profit contribution of his top ten customers.

And while the measuring and managing of customer satisfaction has been getting a lot of attention these days, there is a lot more talking than walking on this subject.

We do about 40 seminars and conferences per year, addressing about 2,500 managers. Each time we ask for a show of hands to see how many work for companies that measure customer satisfaction on a structured and consistent basis. Only about 10% to 15% of the attendees put their hands in the air. And of these, the majority do only surveys with limited samples—once every year or two!

If 90% of the business comes from current customers, doesn't a constant monitoring of satisfaction levels make sense?

These are just some of the symptoms of the Marketing and Sales "black box syndrome."

Let's take a minute or two to examine what's happening with this black box.

Chapter 6

Marketing and Sales: From Black Box to White Box

What would happen if you made these statements to your top management, board of directors, or shareholders?

> "I know that 50% of my production is rejected. But I don't know why."
>
> "I know that 50% of my deliveries are late. But I can't do anything about it."
>
> "I know that 50% of my administration is inaccurate. What a pity."

Admit it: these statements would in no time result in your being downsized or assigned as "Manager of Special Projects" in Prudhoe Bay, Alaska.

But would your career be damaged if you made this statement?

> "I know that 50% of my advertising budget is wasted. The problem is I don't know which 50%."

Until recently, probably not. A man who often said this—Mr. Lever, a founder of Unilever—was anointed Lord Leverhulme. And today his words are sometimes still acceptable to top management, the board of directors, and shareholders.

Why? Simply because, for many companies, marketing and sales have always been a "black box" . . . a budgetary Bermuda Triangle into which large amounts of money are poured without the rigorous process control techniques used to measure and manage the productivity of production, logistic, and administrative processes. (See Figure 6.1.)

Here are some examples of the "black box syndrome":

- Company A, which spends months calculating the ROI prior to purchasing a $50,000 production machine, approves a million-dollar advertising campaign in an afternoon. (The wife of the CEO thinks it is "cute"!)
- Company B, with a sophisticated "just-in-time" logistics flow to manage components costing $50 each, has no system to track field sales force visits that cost $200 each.
- Company C has a perfect invoicing system for billing customers. But they have no idea of how satisfied these customers are with the products or services invoiced.

Why has the box always been so black?

How is it possible for these situations to exist? After talking to a lot of marketing and sales people around the world, we detected three main reasons.

Figure 6.1

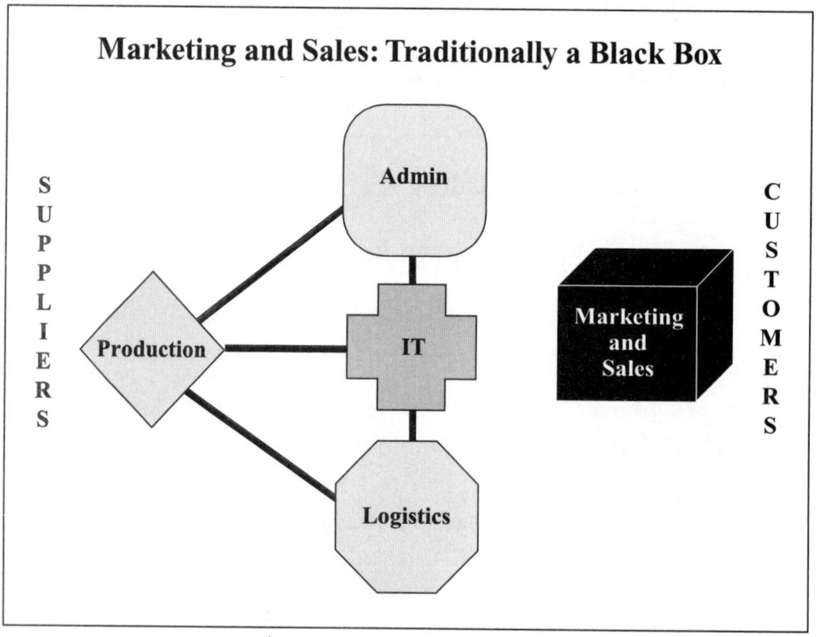

Marketing and Sales: Traditionally a Black Box

SUPPLIERS — Production — Admin — IT — Logistics — Marketing and Sales — CUSTOMERS

1. "Chinese Walls" exist between marketing and sales.

Customers think that marketing and sales are one and the same.

They assume that a mailing to which they respond, resulting in a salesperson's visit, are the activities of one corporate department.

In fact, these two customer contacts usually come from two different departments and are funded by two very different budgets managed by two very different people—the sales manager and the marketing manager. And they may not always be in cooperation mode.

In this situation, calculating the return on investment of a campaign with marketing's mailing and the sales visit is difficult. Calculating the return on marketing and sales budgets that are separate is impossible.

2. The "Dilbert" Syndrome.

The Dilbert comic strip illustrates with great humor the yawning gap in understanding and cooperation between marketing and IT.

One reason is that marketing/sales and IT traditionally have not had much to do with each other. Without a need for marketing and sales metrics, not many companies were making IT investments in this area.

In 1991 my business partner, Wil Wurtz, developed a database full of information about marketing and sales software systems with the idea of helping companies select the right package. A great idea, but at that time it was a bust. Why? Because in 1991 the person most often made responsible for selecting a marketing and sales package was . . . *the student intern!*

Getting back to Dilbert—it is true that IT and marketing/sales people often come from wildly different professional planets. The one was rational and structured; the other, intuitive and less structured.

3. Marketing and sales metrics have never been mandatory.

There have never been any external pressures to measure the productivity and ROI on marketing and sales.

Other departments and processes have one or more "Big Brothers" watching them.

• The financial/administrative departments are required to keep very accurate records required by the Internal Revenue Service, shareholders, and the Securities and Exchange Commission.

• Manufacturing and logistics operations have to pass muster with the inspectors who grant and renew ISO, environmental, safety, and other kinds of certificates needed to stay in business.

As a result, managers are sensitive to the fact that they can be fired, sued, or put in jail if they don't come up with the right numbers at the right time. So management has made sure that the finance, production, and other departments get the right metrics.

But who needs to invest in getting marketing and sales metrics if you get a nod of approval from your peers with a statement like this:

> "I know that 50% of my marketing and sales budget is wasted. I don't know which 50%—and at the end of the day, it doesn't really matter."

Why the black box is becoming white.

The situation sketched above is changing rapidly. The black box of marketing and sales is becoming white, if not transparent.

1. Marketing and sales are merging.

The traditional split between marketing and sales is fading away. An ever-increasing number of companies realize that marketing and sales are two interrelated activities that have the common goal of

• Creating customers
• Keeping customers
• Maximizing customer profitability

As a result, the artificial separation of marketing and sales activities and budgets is fading away, thus making budgets transparent and ROI calculations possible on budget, campaign, and customer levels.

And marketing and sales people are now finding themselves together in an office with "Customer Relationship Management" on the door.

2. "Front Office Systems" is creating a feeding frenzy for IT suppliers.

The fastest-growing software and systems segment today is Front Office Systems. These are hard- and software combinations that help companies deal with their customers.

They come in all kinds of shapes, sizes, colors, and names:

- Contact managers
- Sales force automation
- Call center management
- Datamining
- Data warehousing
- Marketing and sales information systems

and, of course, Customer Relationship Management (CRM) systems.

Why is this happening now? Probably for a complex of reasons:

- Technology that has been cheap and flexible enough to handle masses of transaction data at the customer level.
- A new breed of marketing and sales managers who grew up using computers and started buying gear for their departments.
- The implementation of ERP (Enterprise Resource Planning) systems that (try to) support all company operations, including marketing and sales.
- The wild growth of the Internet and its capability to capture and manipulate customer information. (We will discuss this intensively in Part Three.)

Last but not least, there is a great deal of "technology push" from the IT suppliers themselves. But the result is that there is now a wide range of tools for measuring, managing and improving marketing, sales, and customer processes.

3. Marketing and sales metrics are in vogue.

Marketing and sales accountability is "in." Someone at Volkswagen told us a while ago:

"Señor Lopez is coming to marketing and sales!"

Evidently, this famous and fanatical cost-cutter went about as far as he could by squeezing suppliers to reduce manufacturing costs, introducing "just-in-time" systems to improve logistics, and replacing administrators with software.

But he has noticed that a Volkswagen leaves the factory at price index 50 and is delivered to the consumer at price index 100.

His conclusion: There has to be some room in there to increase Volkswagen's profits through efficiencies in marketing, sales, and distribution.

Customer-based metrics are also in vogue. In the United States, Bain & Co. conducted a survey in 1990 (quoted by just about every speaker on CRM) that showed the dramatic profit increases if customer defection could be reduced by 5%. And in Europe the Customer Based Accounting methods described in this book have been published in five languages.

Finally, the quality movement—and the requirement for ISO certification—has introduced the concept of statistical process control techniques outside production.

Statistical process control is embodied in the cybernetic loop applied by quality control people around the world to production, logistical, and administration activities. It includes these steps (see Figure 6.2):

Figure 6.2

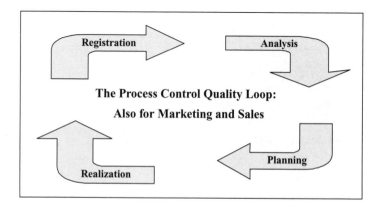

- *Registration* and collection of necessary data on critical factors.
- *Analysis* of the data so you know where you are now.
- *Planning* and budgeting based on the analysis.
- *Realization* of the plans made.
- *Reregistration* by going back into the loop again with remeasurement of the data on the critical factors

Figure 6.3

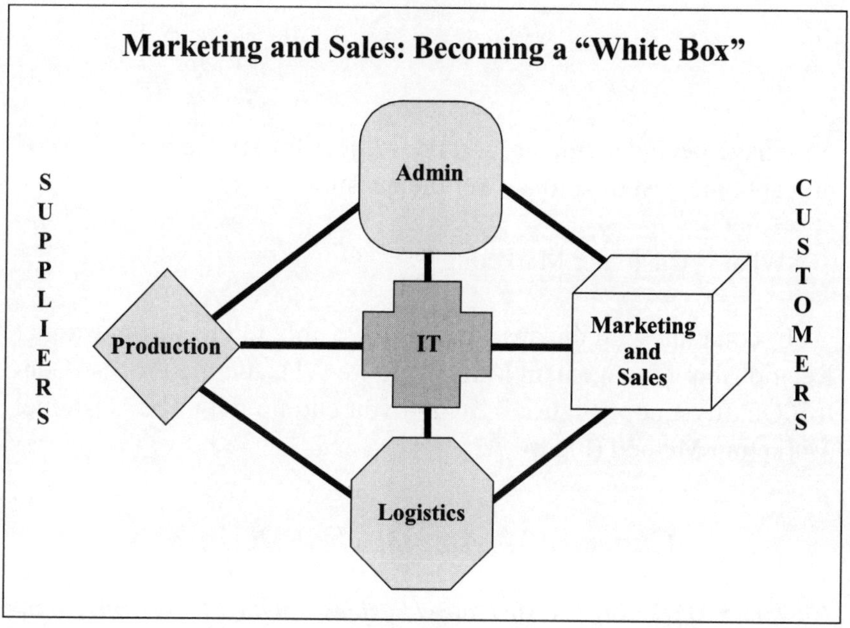

Marketing and Sales: Becoming a "White Box"

In short, marketing and sales is becoming more and more a white box, transparent to those who manage, carry out—and finance—commercial processes (see Figure 6.3).

The Customer Marketing method is "white box" all the way!

Chapter 7

The Customer Marketing Method

We have been dancing around the subject for six chapters. Now is probably the best time to answer the question:

"What is Customer Marketing?"

To come up with the answer, you have only to take the Customer Relationship Management Model (Figure 7.1), add the Process Control Quality Loop (Figure 7.2), and you end up with The Customer Marketing Method (Figure 7.3).

Customer Marketing: The Definition

Customer Marketing is a structured business method to measure, manage, and improve the performance of your customers and the customer focus of your company.

Customer Performance is measured in terms of

- Customer Value
- Customer Behavior
- Customer Satisfaction

Customer Focus Factors Include

- Information
- Communication
- Organization

Figure 7.1

The Customer Relationship Management Model

Customer Marketing: The Metrics

The Customer Marketing method helps you measure and manage Customer Performance and Customer Focus using the following metrics.

You can measure your *Customer Performance* with the following parameters.

Figure 7.2

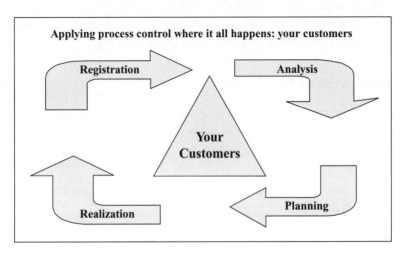

Figure 7.3

Customer Value

- *Profit per Customer*—the bottom line contribution of a customer.
- *Customer Lifetime Value*—the average profit contribution of a customer during the average length of the relationship.
- *Net Present Value*—the sum total of customer lifetime value discounted for the cost of money and other factors.

Customer Behavior

- *Revenue per Customer*—the revenue received from a customer.
- *Customer Share*—the percentage that a customer spends with your company versus the total spent for goods and services in your category.
- *Customer Lifetime*—the length of time a customer maintains a buying relationship with your company.

Customer Satisfaction

- *Satisfaction Scores*—the rating a customer gives to your delivery of products, services, and relationship factors.
- *Loyalty Indicators*—scores indicating whether or not a customer is likely to continue doing business with you.

And you can measure *Customer Focus* with self-assessment or audit scores.

Organization

- *Management*—how your management deals with customers—or doesn't.
- *Staff*—how your employees or colleagues increase—or decrease—customer satisfaction.

Communication

- *Media/Methods/Messages*—what you say to your customers, and how.
- *Contact Logistics*—how you plan and follow up on communications with your customers.

Information

- *Customer Information*—the relevance, completeness, and timeliness of information that you have on your customers.
- *System*—the performance of the system that manages your customer information.

Customer Marketing: The Method

Customer Marketing follows the four quality loop phases discussed earlier and described in detail in Part Two of this book:

Registration

- *Customer Performance Registration:* You acquire or integrate from internal sources data on customer profitability, behavior, and satisfaction.

- *Customer Focus Registration:* You undertake a customer focus audit or self-assessment of your customer information, communications, and organization.

Analysis

- *Customer Performance Analysis:* You analyze the profitability, behavior, and satisfaction of your customers and prospects to identify problems and opportunities.
- *Customer Focus Analysis:* You analyze the current status of your customer information, communications, and organization and identify priorities for improvement.

Planning

- *Customer Performance Planning:* You set top-down/bottom-up profitability, revenue, and satisfaction targets for each customer (and prospect) that, when realized, will meet corporate goals for profitability, revenues, and satisfaction.
- *Customer Focus Planning:* You make plans to make measurable improvements in your customer information, communications, and organization.

Realization

- *Customer Performance Realization:* You execute customer performance plans.
- *Customer Focus Realization:* You execute customer focus plans.

This seems all very rational and scientific. But are CRM and Customer Marketing based only on the numbers?

Chapter 8

Customer Marketing: Not Just the Numbers

It is possible that, after reading the preceding chapters, you may be thinking along these lines:

> Statistical process control techniques? Accountability of marketing and sales? Measure and manage? What am I doing here? It seems like Customer Marketing means we have to staff marketing and sales with a bunch of geeks, nerds, accountants, and efficiency experts armed with stopwatches.

No way. And here are three reasons why.

1. It is very difficult—if not impossible—to train accountants, bookkeepers, and quality control specialists to be marketing managers or salespeople. But it is possible to teach some accounting tricks to marketing and sales people. (I have yet to meet a salesperson who can't figure out the commission he will get for an order he is about to close, no matter how complex the metrics may be.)

2. Customer Marketing does help you come up with some hard numbers on some issues that you heretofore may have considered not measurable, or "soft." But the Customer Marketing metrics do not have to pass Generally Accepted Accounting Practice standards or the steely eyes of a due diligence lawyer. The numbers are working tools for you and your colleagues. So you decide yourself when you have reached an accuracy or reliability level with which you are comfortable.

3. The Customer Marketing method takes into account that marketing, sales, and service people—in fact, everyone who deals with customers—are chock full of creativity, intuition, and ideas, and customers need real-world human interaction, and they thrive on intuition and emotional benefits.

In other words, Customer Marketing appreciates the synergy and value of blending rationality with intuition, left lobe with right lobe, yin with yang.

The following four chapters describe some key elements of Customer Marketing that take full advantage of the creativity, knowledge, and relationship skills of your management and staff:

- Customer Interviews
- Customer Teams
- Top-Down, Bottom-Up Customer Planning
- Company-Wide Participation

Chapter 9

Customer Interviews

Customer interviews—*ideally with each and every one of your customers (and prospects)*—are a critical element of Customer Marketing.

You can conduct these interviews face to face, via the telephone, through written or e-mail questionnaires or via your Web site.

But no matter which method or medium you use for the customer interviews, the payoff will be dramatic.

In fact, your first structured program of customer interviews is likely to be the most important marketing and sales activity you will undertake all year.

Here's why:

• *You will discover the real needs and problems of each customer.* Armed with this knowledge, you will be able to tailor precisely your offers and products and services to meet the customer's needs and solve his problems.

• *You will find out what aspects of your business are not satisfying each customer*—and what things you are doing right. You can then immediately act to fix the problem for the individual customer and, with the aggregated information, improve aspects that seem to be less than satisfactory for many customers. A customer interview can also prevent the defection of a customer. It is not impossible that you will hear something like this: "I am glad you are here so we could straighten out this problem. Because, believe me, I was about to stop buying from you."

• *You will be able to determine the current and future potential of each customer.* Through the use of "funnel questioning," you can drill down to discover current budgets and future plans for purchasing your products and services. And if you do it correctly, you will also learn which of your competitors your customers are doing business with—or are trying to eat your lunch. This information is essential in helping you set realistic targets for each customer and decide how much time to invest in reaching the targets.

• *You will deepen your relationship with each customer.* "Let's talk about me!" is an unspoken wish of just about everyone. The most fascinating topic of conversation for people is themselves and their business. Aside from gaining critical information, the process of asking questions, listening carefully, and responding appropriately will inevitably strengthen your bond with every customer you interview. Normally, a face-to-face customer interview is scheduled to take 45 minutes. But quite often the customers find the experience so positive that they cancel other appointments to continue it for another 45 minutes of "face time" so valuable to you.

• *You will generate additional sales revenues immediately—and in the longer term.* The customer interview is not a sales call. You inform the customer in advance that you want to get his opinions about his industry, his needs, his plans. And you tell him that you will not bring your order book. But quite often, during the interview, the customer will say: "While you are here, let me tell you about a situation that your company may be able to solve." (It's tough to resist the temptation to suspend the interview—but you should suggest that you will come back to the issue when the interview is completed!)

Customer Interview Cases

Let's look at some examples.

Temporary Help Agency

This company identified 1,000 customers in the middle of their pyramid that, because of their industry and size, should have been using their services more often. Each of the 100 managers of the sales offices were assigned 10 customers to interview. Equipped with a structured questionnaire and a training session, the managers got on the telephone, made their appointments, and conducted the interviews.

The results:

• The managers were able to make account plans for each and every customer visited.

• The sales results of the interviewed customers was tracked during the following six months. The revenues of the entire customer base *dropped 8%* because of a sudden and severe recession. But the *revenues from the interviewed customers increased by no less than 6%* in the six-month period.

Clothing Retailer

A discount retailer of clothes primarily for women and children had hundreds of thousands of customers visiting their 10 locations. They didn't know much about their customers and decided to make a start building a customer database.

To get this information, they conducted a "customer interview" in written form by putting a short questionnaire at the cash registers asking customers about family size and ages, satisfaction issues, and preferences for store hours. The promise: If you fill in this questionnaire, we will send you an advance copy of our door-to-door flyers so you can come in and get the bargains before other people.

The results:

• In a matter of weeks, 200,000 "interviews" were completed and the information provided the basis of the long-overdue customer database.

• The normally slow January selling season was given a real boost because the retailer discovered two types of baby clothes buyers:

Type A: women aged 59–99, whom they assumed were grandmothers and godmothers

Type B: women aged 19–49, whom they assumed were mothers

On November 20 they sent a high-quality mailing featuring expensive and exclusive children's clothes to the Type A women, with a signed "personal" letter commenting that they had bought children's clothes in the past and suggesting the offered collection as gift ideas.

On January 2 they sent an inexpensive mailing to Type B women as a post-Christmas sale of fine clothes at reduced prices—resulting in a January revenue increase of more than 20% compared with the year before.

Office Equipment Supplier (Prospect Interviews)

A supplier of photocopy machines wanted to break into a new market for their high-volume machines. Faced with the need for qualified prospects, they used a combination of telephone and written question-naires to interview the person in charge of photocopies in medium to large companies. The promise: The interviewee would get an analysis of copying patterns in his industry, against which he could evaluate his own situation (plus an evening at a health club and the chance to win a weekend vacation . . .). The questions asked:

- How many copies per month are produced in your company?
- How many copying machines were installed in your company?
- What is the brand and model number of your machines?
- What is the expiration date of the rental contract for each machine?

The results:

- *No less than 70%* of the interviewees supplied the required infor-mation.
- The delivery of the report (by the salesperson for qualified prospects) started a large number of sales cycles that resulted in a profitable customer base.

The Cost-Effectiveness of Customer Interviews

Despite hard evidence and the "gut feeling" that customer interviews pay off, some managers have a negative reaction to the idea.

Sometimes financial managers react this way:

> "What? Doing an interview with every customer costs too much money! A telephone interview costs $10 each, and we have 3,000 customers. That's $30,000. No way!"

But when you point out that it costs $360 per customer per year to send invoices (the normal cost is about $30 per monthly invoice), spending $10 to find out whether or not a customer will continue to do business with you is a real bargain.

And sometimes sales managers have an initial reaction like this:

"What? Spending an hour or two with each customer takes too much time! We simply don't have the time to meet with each customer and find out what their needs are and how we can help them solve their problems with our products and services. *We have to go out and sell!*"

But when you point out that a face-to-face customer interview can take place during a normally scheduled sales visit, that with more customer knowledge your sales visit frequency with that customer can be reduced, and that a number of interviews will score an (unexpected) order, then they see the light.

In the second part of this book we will go into the details of customer interviews, questionnaire design, and selection of methods and media for your interviews. But this chapter would not be complete without the story of Jan de Boer and his unique method of customer interviews.

The Customer Marketing Interviews of Jan de Boer

One of the authors was invited to give a speech on Customer Marketing to a group of industrialists. During the before-presentation coffee period one of the attendees approached him and offered his hand.

The man introduced himself as Jan de Boer of De Boer Industries and expressed his thanks. The reason: He had done everything suggested in an early version of this book on Customer Marketing. And it had really worked for him.

His $60,000 Mercedes in the parking lot indicated that he was doing something right. And so he was asked if he would share some of his experiences with the group during the presentation. Jan agreed.

Halfway through the presentation the author invited Jan to reveal his most effective technique for moving customers up his customer pyramid.

Not without a look of pride, Jan de Boer stood up and addressed the group.

"How do I get customers to move up the pyramid? It's really very easy. I always carry my customer pyramid with me. When I visit a small customer, I show him the pyramid and point to his position in the lower layer and say:

"'Sir, this is our customer pyramid. Look, here you are in the bottom section . . .'

"The customer looks at the pyramid and then responds with a worried look:

"'Gee, that's not so good, is it . . .'

"'But maybe it could be better . . . so please tell me this: What can I do to get you higher in the customer pyramid?'

"And then I hear answers like these, which keep me riding in a big new Mercedes:

- "'De Boer, If you can give me 45 days credit instead of 30 days, you get all my business.'
- "'Jan, I have a logistical problem. If you can deliver directly to my customers and spare me the logistics and warehousing costs, you will get many more orders from me.'
- "'Sir, we are a small company and we buy only from you. I'm sorry, but it will take us some time to move up your pyramid . . .'"

Jan de Boer concluded his story with this interesting statement:

"The great thing about these interviews is that the customers *never, ever talk about prices!*"

Would Jan's interview method work for you? Give it a try!

Chapter 10

Customer Teams

"Nobody knows who I am!"

"I keep getting transferred from one department to another!"

"Why don't they communicate with each other?"

These often-heard customer complaints are usually the result of "Stand-Alone" departments, as shown in Figure 10.1.

Some companies try to solve the complaints by "putting the customer on top," as in figure 10.2.

Figure 10.1

"Stand-Alone" Departments

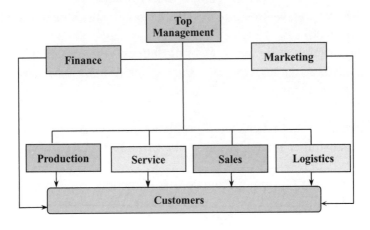

Figure 10.2

"Putting the Customer on Top"

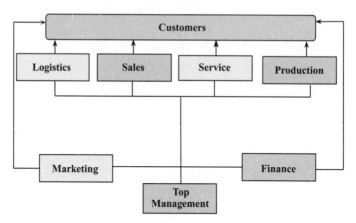

But it doesn't work. The stand-alone departments continue to deal with the customer from their own narrow perspective, leading to customer confusion and anger.

At some companies—certainly not yours—this scenario is not unusual:

> "Buy this product," suggests sales. And the customer agrees.
> "What? You bought this machine? I could have kept the old one going for another year," cries service.
> "It'll take three months to make," says production.
> "What order for what machine?" asks logistics.
> "We love you, we love you!" is the message of the brochure sent by marketing.
> "Pay or Die!" is the message of the letter sent by accounts with the invoice that arrives in the same batch of mail with marketing's love letter.

The answer to this cluster of problems: form Customer Teams!

The Customer Team is a powerful and fundamental Customer Marketing concept.

The primary Customer Team consists of people who have or are responsible for contacts with a specific group of customers, often represented in a customer pyramid.

Figure 10.3

Customer Team

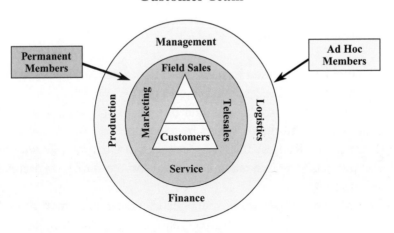

In business-to-business situations, the roster of a Customer Team often looks like this (see Figure 10.3):

- The *Field Sales* person assigned to the customer.
- The *Telesales* person who is "paired" to the Field Sales person or assigned to the customer.
- The *Service Representative* whose route or territory includes the customer.
- A *Marketing* person, who may have responsibility for marketing communications or a product manager who represents the marketing department in the team.

When needed, the Customer Team can be enriched with representatives from other departments, such as finance, research and development (R&D), production, logistics, etc.

How Customer Teams Work

Here is how Customer Teams can work together to improve customer performance.

  • A Customer Manager is assigned to each customer (or prospect). The Customer Manager is responsible for detecting problems and selling opportunities while ensuring that the proper person takes the proper action to achieve the goal.

• While the customer may be under the impression that the Account Manager or Field Sales person is his primary contact person, the Customer Team agrees among themselves that a de facto Customer Manager is assigned to the customer depending on the current customer relationship. For instance:

- The Field Sales person is manager of Customer X because there is a sales cycle in process for a major order.
- The Telesales person is manager of Customer Y, who is a steady customer who normally orders by telephone.
- The Service Representative is manager of Customer Z, who has just purchased a large machine and the service staff is on premises installing it.
- The Marketing person is manager of Suspects, which he will, through telemarketing and direct mail, bring to Prospect status.

The Customer Manager can change if the customer situation changes. For example, if Customer X gives the order and the service staff has to install the machine, the Service Representative becomes Customer Manager. And when a Suspect becomes a qualified Prospect ready to buy, the Field Sales person takes over the account.

Customer Teams do not usually sit and chat in meetings every Monday morning with coffee and donuts. While the teams do meet at critical moments for setting customer goals and making account plans (as described in the following chapter), Customer Teams are quite often "virtual," communicating with each other via e-mail, the telephone, or through activities registered in the customer database system.

Customer Teams: The Payoff

Customer Teams are not formed overnight. They take some time and energy to implement because Account Managers are not always eager to share power or allow other people access to "their" customers. But Customer Teams have proven to be profitable because they can increase sales and customer satisfaction while reducing marketing and sales costs, as you can learn from the following "real world" cases.

Customer Team Case: Health Care

Elizabeth is a salesperson for a company that makes baths for elderly and sick people. She has a trial placement of a bath at a large home for the aged. A trial placement usually means a sale because the product is of very high quality and is already installed on the premises. Elizabeth returns to the customer with her order book in hand, confident of making the sale. But to her dismay, she discovers that, three days earlier, the thermostat on the bath malfunctioned and several old folks narrowly escaped getting cooked. The complaint about the thermostat was reported to service, but Elizabeth didn't know about it.

The result:

• A lost sale, not because of the technical fault, but because the customer lost faith in the company. Elizabeth showed up unaware of the problem. Had there been a Customer Team in place, service would have informed her of the problem, and the order would have been automatic.

Customer Team Case: Flour Miller

A flour miller has a customer (an industrial baker) in the middle of his customer pyramid who is safe and steady, placing orders regularly by telephone. The baker is normally visited by Mike, the Account Manager, eight times a year. Mike takes his customer teammate, Mary of telesales, along with him on a visit to the customer and says this:

"Mr. Customer, we really value your business, so my boss says we should put two people on your account. I am your Account Manager, and you can call me 24 hours a day, seven days a week, if you need me. But I am often on the road. Mary is in the office all day, so for the smaller problems (and the orders!), you can call Mary. As a matter of fact, Mary can call you once each week to see how your stock position is and solve any little problems. Is Tuesday the best day for her to call, or is Thursday better?"

The results:

- The customer was delighted that his importance was recognized and your attention to him doubled.
- Mary can be more efficient by planning her calls to the customer at an agreed-on day and time.
- Mary feels "empowered" with her new responsibilities as Customer Manager.
- Mike can cut his sales visits from eight to five per year, giving him more time to acquire new customers.

Aside from their immediate benefits, Customer Teams also play a key role in the customer planning process, as we will see in the next chapter.

Chapter 11

Top-Down/Bottom-Up
Customer Planning

What goals do you set for your company or business unit for a planning period? Market share? Profits? Profits as a percent of sales? Revenue? Return on investment?

These are all tried-and-true company goals that many managers set in a top-down/bottom-up fashion by looking at last year's numbers, doing some calculations, and setting a preliminary target of, say, 15% more revenues.

The manager then presents this top-down target to the business unit managers or sales managers with the message: "This is what we are going for on the company level next year. What about your group?"

Back come the bottom-up targets, some higher than 15%, others lower. After some negotiations, the boss and his business unit/sales managers reach consensus and commit to hard targets.

Where do all these numbers come from? All too often they are based on historical *sales performance.*

But the inescapable fact of life is that market share, profits, sales, and return on investment come from only one source: *customer performance!*

And this is what Customer Relationship Management is all about: getting customers, keeping customers, and maximizing customer profitability.

From Company Goals to Customer Goals

Thus, you need to translate your corporate goals into *customer goals*. By running some simulations to determine what kinds of customers you need, you can

- identify (get prospects, leads)
- acquire (make a new customer)
- keep (maintain purchasing pattern)
- upgrade (increase purchasing)

to reach your company goal for a given planning period.

Going back to the Ajax Fine Plastics case, you can see that a simulation exercise would have shown them that the net upgrading of 17 customers—while keeping fixed costs equal—would deliver 10% more revenue and 61% more operational profit (see Figure 11.1).

But simulations are quite often divorced from the real world.

You therefore have to drill down at the customer level and determine where you want *each and every customer and prospect* to end up in your customer pyramid at the end of the planning period.

And you can do this customer-based business planning together

Figure 11.1

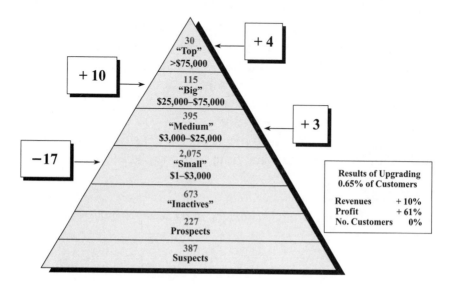

Figure 11.2

Customer Information			Top-Down Customer Goals			
Customer Name	Last Year Revenue	Last Year Pyramid	Behavior Goal	Pyramid Goal	Revenue Target	% Change
Company A	$130,657	Medium	Upgrade	Top	$250,000	91%
Company B	117,940	Medium	Keep	Medium	130,000	10%
Company C	109,845	Medium	Downgrade	Small	15,000	–86%
Result	$358,442				$395,000	10%

with your customer teams to tap into their creativity and their customer knowledge, which is stored away in their heads.

It is very much a top-down, bottom-up process.

Top-Down Customer Goals

The spreadsheet will list scores for hundreds and sometimes thousands of customers and prospects from all layers in the pyramid. But to show a simple example, Figure 11.2 is a spreadsheet with top-down customer goals to meet the goal of a 10% revenue increase of three customers, all of which are in the "Medium" layer of the customer pyramid.

You can see that the statistical analysis indicated that Company A should be upgraded to "Top" status, Company B will remain in the "Medium" layer, and Company C will continue a downward trend and end up as a "Small" customer.

The last thing you can expect is that a customer team will accept top-down customer goals like these without question—especially if they have been produced on a computer operated by a 25-year-old marketing staff nerd!

- They will claim—rightly—that they know more about their customers than some computer nerd who has never gone out and talked to them.
- It is only human to set up resistance against anything that comes "top-down."

So why not let the customer teams first make "bottom-up" customer goals?

This may be possible once the teams have experience with the process. But it is not possible the first time, because sales and marketing people tend to set customer goals *to meet their quota* rather than on the basis of *customer potential.*

Think about the anecdote cited earlier about the IT company that only had less than $5,000 in revenues from KLM for the past two years.

Why had the salesperson on the KLM account not scored bigger orders? Certainly not because of a lack of potential.

The chances are that the salesperson was not comfortable serving such a large customer . . . or didn't know how to penetrate the account further . . . or perhaps put too much time and energy in low-potential customers and prospects where quota could be reached, leaving "no time available" for KLM, which had high potential but a low scoring chance.

The main purpose, then, of top-down customer goals is to help the customer teams and the sales force identify real opportunities to meet and exceed quota by getting them to focus on customers and prospects with real potential.

But the first time you present the top-down customer goals, it may well take the form of a confrontation. Tact, patience, and understanding are required.

Bottom-Up Customer Goals

For starters, you don't send out the top-down customer goal spreadsheet as an attachment to an e-mail that reads: "Here are your customer goals for next year. Meet them."

Instead, you call a meeting of the customer team and explain the techniques used to develop the top-down customer goals to meet the company goal of a 10% revenue increase.

You then say:

"These customer goals come from statistical calculations and, of course, need to be adjusted by you. After all, you certainly know more about your customers than any computer or any nerd at headquarters. But isn't it interesting to see an indication that we could just about double our business with Company A? Anyway, please come back next Friday with what you think you will get from each customer in your territory."

Figure 11.3

Customer Information			Bottom-Up Customer Goals			
Customer Name	Last Year Revenue	Last Year Pyramid	Behavior Goal	Pyramid Goal	Revenue Target	% Change
Company A	$130,657	Medium	Keep	Medium	$150,000	15%
Company B	117,940	Medium	Upgrade	Top	220,000	87%
Company C	109,845	Medium	Downgrade	Small	15,000	–86%
Result	**$358,442**				**$385,000**	**7%**

The customer team is then empowered to review the top-down goals and targets for each customer and come back with their bottom-up customer goals and targets, like those shown in Figure 11.3.

The bottom-up goals show that the people in the "real world" doubt Customer A can be moved to "Top" position but are optimistic about Company B. They concur that Company C will drop to a "Small" position in the customer pyramid.

To your dismay, they also forecast a growth of only 7% among these customers, below the company goal of 10%.

Consensus and Commitment Customer Goals

The shortfall in projected sales revenue can usually be resolved by negotiation and management "encouragement." In this case, consensus on the goals achieved—and the commitment to realize them—was reached in a short time (see Figure 11.4).

Top-Down/Bottom-Up Contact Plans

It's one thing to set goals for each customer and prospects. It's another thing entirely to "make it happen" with marketing and sales activities or customer contacts.

The logical consequence: You need to make and execute a contact plan for each and every customer and prospect to reach the goal.

And to increase customer profitability, the contact plan should contain a mix of methods and media that can achieve the goal at *a minimum cost.*

Figure 11.4

Customer Information			Consensus and Commitment Customer Goals			
Customer Name	Last Year Revenue	Last Year Pyramid	Behavior Goal	Pyramid Goal	Revenue Target	% Change
Company A	$130,657	Medium	Keep	Medium	$150,000	15%
Company B	117,940	Medium	Upgrade	Top	230,000	95%
Company C	109,845	Medium	Downgrade	Small	15,000	–86%
Result	**$358,442**				**$395,000**	**10%**

As Figure 11.5 illustrates, you can select from various methods, media or technologies (face-to-face, telephone, print, and electronic) that are delivered on an individual, one-on-one basis or are delivered to specified groups.

Face-to-face and individual contacts have the highest effect—and also the highest cost.

For instance, a sales visit by a top manager can cost up to $400—but there is no more powerful customer contact than the Managing Director visiting a customer with the Account Manager (add another $200 to the cost of the visit!), who just comes along to ask (like Jan de Boer): "How's business and what can we do for you?"

Figure 11.5

Methods and Media for Contact Plans

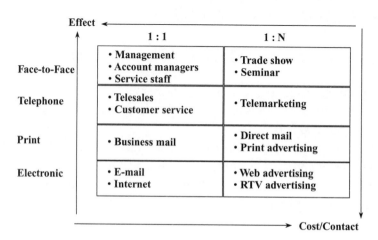

On the other hand, a radio spot sent out in rush hour that reaches thousands of drivers in a traffic jam might not deliver much response. But the cost is only a few pennies per contact.

The mix of methods must be tailored to the individual customer/ prospect situation and the goal or target set for that customer/ prospect.

Let's say you are trying to *create new customers* for your Widgets. You can use your sales force to call companies to find out if they have a Widget; identify the decision maker; try to get a sales appointment; make the sales call; and close the deal.

You'll make some sales, of course. But given the high cost of a salesperson and the limited amount of sales time the person has (often less than 50% of their time on the job!), you may want to consider a different mix of media and methods that delivers more new customers, more sales, and at a lower cost per sale:

- *Outbound telemarketing* to see if the suspect company has a Widget, identify Widget decision maker
- *Direct mail* to the Widget decision makers to generate sales leads
- *Internal sales force call* to qualify the leads and make appointments for a demonstration
- *External sales force* to give the demonstration, create the customer, close the sale
- *Outbound telemarketing* to nonrespondents to make appointment for a demonstration

In the case of *current customers,* you can substitute some routine sales visits (costing $200 in sales time) with programmed telephone calls ("business calls") by the salespeople (costing $20 each in sales time). The customer will appreciate the service, while the cost of the customer contact is reduced by $180. If the customer places an order over the telephone—which happens more often than you may think— the cost of the sale is a mere $20. And the salesperson has more time to create new customers. (Strangely enough, some companies do not count a "business call" as an effective customer contact—even though, when combined with face-to-face visits, it may be one of the most profitable selling methods in the company. Only face-to-face visits count as a customer contact.)

Surely there is a need for making contact plans for different customer and prospect situations. And again the question may be asked: Why not start with bottom-up contact plans?

In fact, most companies work with bottom-up contact plans, because most sales managers leave it to the salespeople to decide how often and when they will visit their assigned customers and prospects.

But what criteria do the salespeople use for deciding which customer or prospect to visit? The potential of the customer or prospect? Of course. But not always.

Other factors play a role in the salesperson's mind when making a decision whom to visit and when:

- Will I score an order?
- Will I come out of here looking good?
- Do these people like me?
- Do they serve Danish with the coffee?
- Will Irene or Bob be at the reception desk when I get there?

You would never give a customer/prospect list to a mailing house and let them decide to whom they will send mailings at $2 per piece. And you would never allow the telemarketing agency to decide whom they will call at $15 per call.

But who decides whom a salesperson will visit at a cost of $100 to $700 per visit? The salesperson, of course.

What's the result? A major office equipment company discovered that their salespeople spent 50% of their visits on the 80% "Small" customers, who were delivering only 20% of the revenues and a net loss on the bottom line. Small was evidently beautiful for the salespeople.

On the other hand, field sales, telesales, and other customer team members do know the customers and prospects better than anyone else. So it is essential to make top-down plans that make specific suggestions for allocating their time and resources and then allow them to come back with bottom-up alternatives—within the limits of their time and budgets.

Top-Down Contact Plans

Top-down contact plans are made to resolve the issue of who does what to which customer and prospect in the most cost-effective way. It happens like this:

Figure 11.6

Customer Situation			Standard Contact Plans				
Last Year Pyramid	Behavior Goal	Pyramid Goal	Sales Visits	Business Calls	Catalog Mailings	Show Invite	Football Tickets
Medium	Keep	Medium	6	4	4	1	1
Medium	Upgrade	Top	8	8	4	1	1
Medium	Downgrade	Small	4	4	4	1	0

Figure 11.7

Consensus and Commitment Customer Goals				Top-Down Contact Plans				
Customer Name	Last Year Pyramid	Pyramid Goal	Revenue Target	Sales Visits	Business Calls	Catalog Mailings	Show Invite	Football Tickets
Company A	Medium	Medium	$150,000	6	4	4	1	1
Company B	Medium	Top	230,000	8	8	4	1	1
Company C	Medium	Small	15,000	4	4	4	1	0
Result			$395,000	18	16	12	3	2

Marketing and sales normally sit down together (yes, it happens!) to share information on their budgets for money and capacity: how many sales visits and business calls can the sales force make next year; how many catalogs will be printed and mailed; when is the trade show; and how many football game tickets will be allocated to customers and prospects (and the account managers going with them to the game).

Then, with their wisdom and experience, they make "Standard Contact Plans" for each possible client situation.

For the sake of clarity and simplicity, we will use the customer situations as shown in the customer goals discussion above.

As you can see in Figure 11.6, marketing and sales management concluded that keeping a "Medium" customer at the medium level required a time and money investment of six sales visits, four business calls and catalog mailings, a trade show invitation, and a ticket to the football game. The "Medium" customer migrating to "Top" required more time and energy, and the one targeted for downgrade, less.

The Standard Contact Plans were then, in the spreadsheet, coupled to actual customers in each of the customer situations, which were the

Figure 11.8

Consensus and Commitment Customer Goals				Bottom-Up Contact Plans				
Customer Name	Last Year Pyramid	Pyramid Goal	Revenue Target	Sales Visits	Business Calls	Catalog Mailings	Show Invite	Football Tickets
Company A	Medium	Medium	$150,000	8	6	4	1	1
Company B	Medium	Top	230,000	8	6	4	1	1
Company C	Medium	Small	15,000	2	4	4	1	1
Result			$395,000	18	16	12	3	3

output of the customer goal planning exercise (see Figure 11.7).

Again, tact, patience, and understanding are required in presenting top-down contact plans for the first time to the customer teams. Consider a dialogue something like this:

> "You did a great job with making the customer goals for the people in your customer pyramid. But now we have to figure out how to 'make it happen.' Marketing and sales have come up with some contact planning ideas on this spreadsheet. Once again, you guys know the customers out there better than anyone else. So please take three days to come back with what you think you should be doing in each of these customer situations."

Bottom-Up Contact Plans

Because of your motivational skills and charismatic leadership, the customer team or sales group will return with their bottom-up contact plan.

Notice that the bottom-up plan in Figure 11.8 readjusted the mix of sales visits and business calls and agreed with the allocation of catalog mailings and trade show invitations. But the customer team wanted to allocate a football ticket to Company C "because the buyer is such a nice guy."

A problem: Football tickets were in short supply. So after some "discussion," it was agreed that the Company C buyer would be invited out to lunch and given the "De Boer" treatment to see if he could commit to keeping his buying at the same level. If he committed, he would get the ticket.

Figure 11.9

Consensus and Commitment Customer Goals				Consensus and Commitment Contact Plans				
Customer Name	Last Year Pyramid	Pyramid Goal	Revenue Target	Sales Visits	Business Calls	Catalog Mailings	Show Invite	Football Tickets
Company A	Medium	Top	$150,000	8	6	4	1	1
Company B	Medium	Medium	230,000	8	6	4	1	1
Company C	Medium	Small	15,000	2	4	4	1	0
Result			**$395,000**	**18**	**16**	**12**	**3**	**2**

Consensus and Commitment Contact Plans

Pending the results of the lunch with Company C, this contact plan was agreed on and the team made the commitment to carry it out.

And with consensus and commitment on both customer goals and contact plans, the process of customer-based business planning was complete!

With Customer Marketing, the top-down/bottom-up process is not limited to marketing, sales, and customer teams. Everybody needs to get involved.

Chapter 12

Company-Wide Involvement

Who are the real experts in your company on the subject of what your customers are doing and thinking about you?

Sales, marketing, and service people, to be sure. But they have no monopoly on customer knowledge.

Old Joe worked 40 years at a publishing company processing new subscribers and handling cancellations for a trade magazine for the fashion industry.

Joe remarked laconically to a colleague one day: "We had a lousy issue of the fashion magazine last week."

"What didn't you like about it?" asked the visitor.

Joe replied: "Oh, I never read that magazine. The subscribers—they told me all about it."

Here he was, a man with 40 years of customer contacts with new and departing subscribers. But nobody from the editorial or subscription departments had ever tapped into his knowledge.

Customer Relationship Management is too important to be left to marketing and sales.

Company-wide participation is essential because

• *Everyone in the company can improve customer profitability.* It took a while, but old Joe was trained, when a subscriber canceled a subscription, to say these magic words: "Gee, that's too bad. Why are you canceling?" If he heard, "It's too expensive!" Joe would look at his computer and say, "I see you are paying the full price. With a multiyear subscription you get a 33% discount. I'll just put you down for this special deal." His conversions to the three-year subscription were very profitable.

• *Everyone in the company can improve customer behavior.* The courier for an international express parcel company saw in a customer mailroom stacks of documents for local delivery to be picked up by a competitor. He mentioned to the mail room superintendent that his company also did local deliveries and that by combining both local and international shipments he'd have one-stop shopping with less administration. The mail room supervisor replied: "I want to know more. Have the account guy call me." The result—bingo!

• *Everyone in the company can improve customer satisfaction.* The clerk in bookkeeping heard complaints from her counterpart on the client side that the invoices were difficult to interpret—and people were getting angry about the situation. She reported this up the line. Her boss designed a new invoice format to fix the problem. And the account manager contacted the customer to thank them for their advice (and to demonstrate a new product).

It goes without saying, however, that these happy cases can go the opposite direction.

• *Everyone in the company can decrease customer profitability.* Old Joe can passively accept cancellations.

• *Everyone in the company can decrease customer behavior.* The courier can arrive late for the pick-up and the order is given to a competitor.

• *Everyone in the company can decrease customer satisfaction.* The clerk in bookkeeping can get into an argument with her counterpart on the client side.

There are a number of techniques to tap into and use the customer knowledge of everyone in the company, which will be discussed in Part Two. In the meantime, here are some activities that have proven successful in raising the customer focus of all hands.

- Start implementing Customer Marketing with a "kick-off" meeting for all hands during which you introduce the concept of the method and demonstrate the customer pyramid.
- Hold regular "Pyramid Meetings" during which you show the migration of customers up, down, in, and out of your pyramids.
- Invite all hands to participate in a Customer Focus.
- Publish or present the results of customer satisfaction surveys and invite suggestions for improvement.
- Set up a suggestion box for improving customer satisfaction. Take

these seriously. Offer a small reward for *every* suggestion and select the best one in the year for a substantial prize or bonus.

You will be amazed at the quantity and quality of the ideas, suggestions, and advice that your real customer experts can come up with. Ask them—and see for yourself!

Chapter 13

Customer Marketing: "What's in It for Me?"

Having spent some time with this book learning about Customer Marketing, you should, rightly, demand an answer to this question: "What's in it for me?"

Here are the four key benefits that one or more aspects of Customer Marketing can deliver.

1. More revenues and profits

By focusing on keeping good (high-revenue/high-profit) customers, you can increase sales without increasing marketing and sales budgets. The result: higher profits. A major drug company reported these results after implementing Customer Marketing in a group selling an antibiotic drug to hospitals:

Situation	Before Customer Marketing	After Customer Marketing
Market Growth	+ 2%	+2%
Sales Revenues	+ 2%	+10%
Sales Visits to Hospitals	1,300	1,300

What led to the *five-fold* increase in revenues?

Situation	Before Customer Marketing	After Customer Marketing
No. Hospitals visited	131	92

Customer Marketing helped this company focus on the right customers/prospects to visit and invest in while keeping in touch with the others via mailings and staying alert for buying signals.

2. Increased customer satisfaction

Unsatisfied customers cost money. You lose the revenue, and it costs a lot of money to replace a customer. A major player in the express package delivery business implemented customer teams not long ago. They measured the percentage of "Highly Satisfied Customers" before and after the customer team implementation program. Figure 13.1 shows the results.

Notice that the customers observed that the only downward trend was frequency of sales contact, a result of sales visits decreasing because service took over some of these from sales. But overall, the increase in customer satisfaction was excellent.

Figure 13.1

Percentage of Highly Satisfied Customers (per issue)

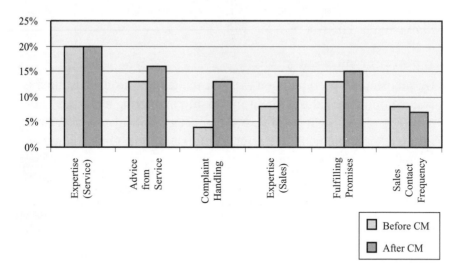

3. More employee motivation

The same case provided empirical evidence about the increase of employee motivation as a result of implementing customer teams. Figure 13.2 shows the results of a before/after survey of customer team implementation among the employees.

There was an improvement across the board.

Figure 13.2

Percentage of Highly Satisfied Employees (per issue)

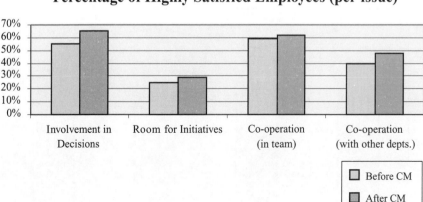

4. Marketing and sales accountability

Customer Marketing equips you with the ways and means to calculate the profitability of individual customers or customer segments, your return on investment on marketing and sales activities, the satisfaction of your customers, and the level of customer focus inside your company. You may not always like the numbers you get in the beginning. But these numbers tell you where you are and point the way for improvement.

If you are still questioning whether or not Customer Marketing will pay off for you, here is a quick test to help you make the decision.

Below are four "statements" about the activities of companies that have implemented Customer Marketing. For each "statement" you can evaluate your own situation by determining the degree to which

• the item applies to your company.
• improvement in this area would help you reach your business goals.

Scoring is as follows:

5 = This statement is absolutely true.
4 = This statement is more or less true.
3 = This statement is equally true and false.
2 = This statement is more or less false.
1 = This statement is absolutely false.

Figure 13.3

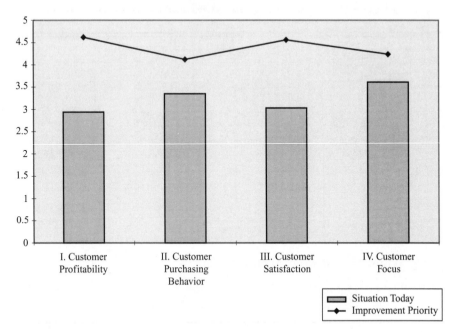

Try it out!

I. We work at measuring and improving the profitability of every customer.
   a. This is the situation at our company today.   1 2 3 4 5
   b. Improvement in this area would help us achieve our business goals.   1 2 3 4 5

II. We work at measuring and improving the purchasing behavior of every customer.
   a. This is the situation at our company today.   1 2 3 4 5
   b. Improvement in this area would help us achieve our business goals.   1 2 3 4 5

III. We work at measuring and improving the satisfaction of every customer.
   a. This is the situation at our company today.   1 2 3 4 5
   b. Improvement in this area would help us achieve our business goals.   1 2 3 4 5

IV. We work at measuring and improving the customer focus of our company's organization, communications, and information.

a. This is the situation at our company today.   1 2 3 4 5

b. Improvement in this area would help us achieve our business goals.   1 2 3 4 5

Check your scores. Are there substantial gaps between your situation today and your improvement priorities? (See Figure 13.3.)

If so, go on to Part Two of this book, which helps you implement
everything you have read about so far—and more!

Part Two

How to Implement CRM with Customer Marketing in Your Company or Business Unit

Part One of this book described the Customer Marketing method as a way to help managers put Customer Relationship Management into practice and allow them to say:

> "The true business of *our* company is to make customers, keep customers, and maximize customer profitability."

But you may well be thinking something like this:

> "Customer Marketing. Yeah, right. Looks logical. But how can I make it happen in *my* company?"

Part Two of the book describes a step-by-step, phased approach for implementing Customer Marketing that has been tried, tested, and proved effective.

Phase I. Preparation

I. A. Make Your Customer Pyramid

- Define your customers and their "customer behavior variables."
- Gather and sort the behavior variables for all your customers.
- Fix your customer pyramid segment "borders" and . . . there you have it!

I. B. Keep Project Management Simple

- Make the Management Team a Steering Committee.
- Select an optimal model project area.

- Appoint a strong Project Manager.
- Install a Customer Marketing Project Group.

I. C. Conduct a Parameters Workshop

- Show and discuss the Customer Pyramid.
- Specify your objectives.
- Define your "value propositions."
- Define total spend (factors).
- Define customer share (factors).
- Conduct a "Customer Information Quick Scan":
  - Basic information.
  - "DMU" information.
  - Customer financials.
  - Customer behavior variables.

Phase II: Diagnosis

II. A. Conduct Interviews with a Selection of Customers (and Prospects).

- Make a "customer selection."
- Construct your customer interview questionnaire.
- Interview the customer selection.

II. B. Diagnose the Value of Your Customers.

- Determine operational profit.
- Identify all your marketing and sales costs.
- Calculate your average per-customer revenue and profit and your marketing and sales ROI (Return on Investment).
- Allocate margins and costs to customer pyramid segments.
- Analyze customer value per customer pyramid segment.
- Calculate the profitability of individual customers.
- Try "What-if?" scenarios with a planning matrix.
- Make and distribute a customer pyramid with CBA results.

II. C. Diagnose the Behavior of Your Customers.

- Combine customer interview data with the other "Quick Scan" information.
- Make an historical migration matrix.

- Check your customer statistics.
- Verify the feasibility of your "what-if?" scenarios.

II. D. Diagnose the Satisfaction of Your Customers.

- Analyze aggregated scores: Core Product Satisfaction.
- Analyze aggregated scores: Value Propositions.
- Analyze aggregated scores: Loyalty Indicators.
- Analyze Individual Customer Scores.

II. E. Diagnose Your Customer Focus.

- Undertake a Customer Focus Self-Assessment.
- Analyze your customer focus scores and "gaps" to identify improvement priorities.

Phase III: Decisions

- Set up a Customer Scorecard.
- Get CRM advice from the experts.
- Decide go/no go on rollout.
- Decide for which customer satisfaction and customer focus issues improvement groups should be installed.
- Decide how, when and where to organize the key activities of the rollout phase.
- Decide on customer teams composition.
- Schedule rollout phase activities.

Phase IV: Rollout

IV. A. Start with a "Customer Marketing Kick-off."

IV. B. Customer-Based Business Planning Workshop.

- Part I: Set top-down goals for every customer and prospect.
  - Set top-down company goals.
  - Set customer goals for every customer and prospect.
- Part II: Set top-down standard contact plans for every customer and prospect.
  - Budget your contact capacity and costs.
  - Make a "Standard Contact Plan" for every customer/prospect situation.
  - Calculate your "Standard Contact Plan" capacity.

IV. C. Customer Team Workshops

- Session I: Registration.
  - Take it easy at first.
  - Homework: A customer interview.

- Session II: Analysis.
  - Evaluation and review of "homework": customer interviews.
  - Present—and justify—your top-down customer goals.
  - Homework: bottom-up customer goals.

- Session III: Planning.
  - Evaluation and review of "homework": bottom-up customer goals.
  - Present—and justify—your top-down contact plans.
  - Homework: Bottom-up customer goals.

- Session IV: Realization.
  - Evaluation and review of "homework": bottom-up contact plans.
  - Assign customer managers.
  - Put the appointments in the agenda.
  - Don't forget coaching!

IV. D. Monitor Rollout Results.

- Monitor customer value results.
- Monitor customer behavior results.
- Monitor customer contact results.
- Monitor customer satisfaction results.
- Monitor customer focus results.

Phase V: Audit

V. A. Re-measure Results.

- Re-measure customer behavior results.
- Re-measure customer contact results.
- Re-measure customer satisfaction results.
- Re-measure customer focus results.

V. B. Analyze Results.

- Identify what went right.
- Identify what went wrong.
- Revise procedures and processes as required.

You can also get some additional practical tips and tools by clicking to *www.customermarketing.com.*

But before getting down to business, here are some general guidelines based on the implementation experiences of others who endured the arrows while pioneering through the learning curve.

Start with a "model project."

Unless you have a very small company, you should start with a "model project." A model project is a small-scale Customer Marketing implementation project undertaken in a business unit or sales region before it is rolled out company wide.

Sounds like a "pilot project"? Well it's the same thing but with a different name. Why? Because a pilot project often implies, "We will try it out in this small unit first, but if it doesn't work, we won't go further." But if you call it a "model project," the message to everyone is this: "We are committed to a CRM strategy, and the model project will help us learn the best way to implement it in our entire company."

There are two kinds of model projects:

1. *"Vertical" model project:* The Customer Marketing method is put into effect during a few months, as described in this section. The lessons learned, procedures, and materials from the project are then transferred to other business units.
2. *"Horizontal" model project:* Even while you are operating a vertical model project, you can have a number of business units getting familiar with Customer Marketing by having them all do one or two things, such as building a customer pyramid or conducting customer interviews.

Don't wait until your customer database (system) is "ready" for Customer Marketing.

A good customer information system, contact manager, or customer database is essential for Customer Marketing. So if you don't have a (good) customer database and system, you will be tempted to delay a model project until you have a new or improved system up and running.

Don't wait! Start now! You can conduct a Customer Marketing model project with only two items:

1. A spreadsheet on which you have can put . . .
2. A list of your customers with their revenues for one or (preferably) two financial reporting periods.

In fact, you are better off starting a Customer Marketing model project before you even start building or shopping for a new or improved customer database or sales force automation package. Depending on whose report you read, between 50% and 70% of marketing and sales automation projects do not meet their objectives and expectations.

One of the key reasons for these failures is that management, seeking to make marketing and sales more productive, installs *software,* hoping that it will result in a *systematic way of working.* It doesn't work that way. First you need to install the systematic way of working, then find the software to support it. The model project will help you find or develop the right software.

- *You will define your information and system needs.*
  At the end of your model project, you will have a very clear idea of what kinds of customer information you need to store and the desired functions of an ideal marketing and sales automation system for your company. This will allow you to describe in an RFP what you want from your IT department or a systems supplier.

- *You will do it first "on paper."*
  "If you can't do it on paper, you can't do it in the computer" is a bit of wisdom from IT old-timers that still holds true. By using the spreadsheet as a basic tool during the model project, you and everyone else involved will often be working with user-friendly pieces of paper. Working with the paper will focus your mind on the method, not how it is automated. And you won't be distracted by technical problems and systems that are "down."

Of course, working with a spreadsheet is clumsy and slow. And at the end of the model project, your Customer Marketing processes will need to be supported by flexible, powerful, and user-friendly software. But by then you will know what kind of software you need—and the people involved, instead of resisting a new system as a kind of watch-dog, will be clamoring for one!

Expect and prepare to meet some normal resistance to change.

Have you ever been involved with implementing change programs like Total Quality Management, ISO certification, or Business Process Re-engineering? Or read the Dilbert cartoon series? Then you know that change in an organization or working methods can meet with resis-tance. Customer Marketing implementation does not usually require any changes in the organizational diagram. But the way in which the people in the different boxes deal with each other can be improved (read changed).

For instance, Customer Teams mean that field sales, inside sales, and service people work closely together, with one person being "customer manager." The introduction of top-down goals and mea-surability is not always greeted with shouts of joy by field sales-people. You can therefore expect some normal resistance to change with the implementation of Customer Marketing. But you can also prepare to minimize or resolve any resistance by preparing for it in this way:

- *Management must walk the talk.* Customer Marketing and CRM implementation require management commitment that is visible to everyone in the whole company. Sending a memo announcing the program and allocating a budget are not enough. Management has to walk the talk by

  - Getting personally involved in the model project, meeting reg-ularly with the project team, attending workshop sessions, etc.
  - Setting an example. You can't expect employees to take "cus-tomer intimacy" very seriously if top management park their cars closer to the front entrance than the customers who visit your office.
  - Backing up middle managers (sales, marketing, and service), who are on the firing line and have to deal firsthand with any resistance.

- *Equip middle management.* It is middle management—sales, marketing, service—who are the people who actually implement Customer Marketing and CRM in the real world. They are on the firing line, directly confronted with resistance to change. They therefore need to be equipped and prepared to deal with it. You need to make sure that middle managers

  - Know more about Customer Marketing than the people they supervise before the model project begins.
  - Play an active role in making the plans for the model project.
  - Get training and coaching on the subject "How to manage change."
  - Have assurance that they will get the support and backing of top management in resolving any resistance "challenges."

Introducing InterTech

To explain and illustrate Customer Marketing implementation, we will follow the progress of "InterTech," a fictitious company located in the Midwest.

The InterTech patterns of customer value, behavior, and satisfaction have been drawn from numerous actual companies that have been looked at and analyzed closely for more than ten years. And the status of customer focus inside InterTech—the organization, communications, and information—is very representative of companies that have been subjected to customer focus audits.

InterTech is not a very large company, employing 87 people. But it has many of the characteristics of a business unit of a larger business-to-business company.

InterTech is a distributor of electronic and mechanical components. Its customers are manufacturers or assemblers of consumer products (washing machines) and industrial machinery. The company has a central warehouse and four sales and service offices located around the country.

InterTech had $10 million in revenues last year, with an operational profit of just about $500,000. These numbers are not satisfactory to the InterTech owner and CEO, Eric Dines, whose grandfather started the business in the early 1950s.

Stimulated by articles, books, and seminars offered by front-end systems suppliers on "customer intimacy" and "Customer Relationship Management," Eric Dines decided that InterTech, traditionally a technically oriented company, should start becoming a customer-oriented company.

And so he decided to implement CRM following the five phases of the Customer Marketing method represented in Figure II.1.

Figure II.1

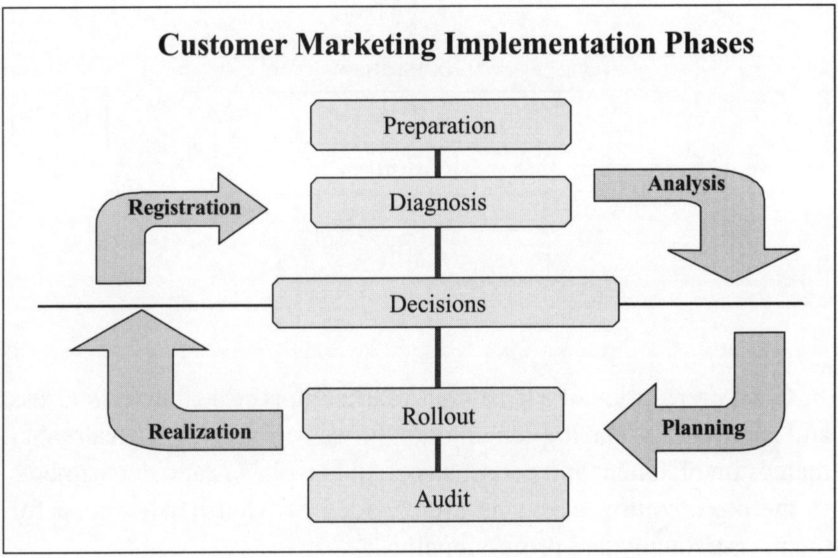

Customer Marketing Implementation Phases

- Preparation
- Diagnosis
- Registration
- Analysis
- Decisions
- Realization
- Rollout
- Planning
- Audit

The rest of this section of the book tells the InterTech story—and helps you write your own!

Phase I: Preparation

Figure II.2

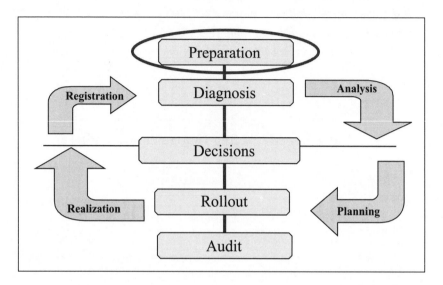

Good preparation of a Customer Marketing is critical to the success and continuity of the implementation process. You have to ensure that there is involvement and consensus of all key players and departments in the organization based on a clear idea of what it will mean for them—personally and professionally.

Make Your Customer Pyramid

Making your first customer pyramid is a reality check.

If you can't come up with a list of customers with their revenues or some other kind of behavior variable for one or two years or other planning periods, you should probably go back to the drawing board. Or at least don't get everyone excited in your company about Customer Marketing implementation until you are certain you can make a customer pyramid within a few weeks.

Define your customers and their "customer behavior variable."

As discussed in Part One, defining who your customer is and structuring your customer pyramid may not be readily obvious. Is your customer the wholesaler? The end user? Or both? You also have to consider what "customer behavior variable" you want to use to structure your customer pyramid, such as revenue (most used) or number of products or services sold. Whatever you choose, your customer behavior variable should be one that you can influence by your marketing, sales, and service activities. Finally, you should decide how long a customer can go without taking action before it is considered inactive. (For companies selling bulldozers, a customer who doesn't order within three years is still considered active. For express parcel companies, a regular customer who doesn't place an order in three or four weeks is considered inactive.)

Eric Dines decided to define InterTech active customers *as decision-making units within a client company that were authorized to*

*write a purchase order. Sometimes a customer was a company.
In other instances, a company could have within its offices several
customers, each of which could write a purchase order indepen-
dently.*

*The customer behavior variable was an easy call: invoiced rev-
enues.*

Inactive customers *he defined as customers who had not purchased goods and services for 12 or more months.*

Gather and sort the behavior variables for all your customers.

These numbers are hard to come by in a retail or fast-mover situation
in which transactions per customer are not registered. You may have to
work with samples of customers and count store visits instead of revenues.

Getting sales revenues per customer data in business-to-business
situations is also not always easy—even if invoices are sent out for
each purchase.

For instance, bookkeeping records may show 12 different customer
numbers at one company. This may be because there is only one customer at that company but the company named is typed in 12 different ways.

Or it may be that there are 12 different business units at the company, each of which is authorized to purchase your products and services and is therefore a different customer.

Usually it is a combination of the two situations. And so there is
no substitute for getting from bookkeeping a list of customers and
their purchases over the year, loading it into Excel or Lotus 1-2-3, and
consolidating the data based on knowledge in the heads of sales, service, and administrative people who know the customer.

Once you have the customer behavior data in a spreadsheet, you
can then rank your customers from top to bottom.

The result is a "customer sort"—a list of customers for the past
year with their sales revenues over a given period.

*Eric called Fred Ramselaar from bookkeeping into his office.
Fred, hired originally by Eric's father, had been with InterTech for
years and had been able to make the transition from punch cards*

to PCs. He also had great knowledge about every customer because he was highly skilled—and persuasive—in chasing after unpaid invoices.

Eric asked him to put all the customers from the Midwest region on a spreadsheet with revenue figures from the past two years—and got him to promise to keep "their little project" confidential. (The reason for his choice of the Midwest region will become clear later.)

In less than a week Fred handed over the spreadsheet to Eric, not without a little pride. Eric then sorted the list for the last year in descending order and, using a rolling cumulative for revenues, calculated the percentages on customers and revenues. You can see the fruits of his efforts in Appendix A. (The names of the InterTech customers have been omitted for competitive and privacy reasons!)

Fix your customer pyramid segment "borders" and . . . there you have it!

Building the customer pyramid is not such a problem when you have a "customer sort." You then have to decide how you will segment your active customers and set the "borders" of the pyramid accordingly. (Inactive customers are easy to find: they are on the books—but without any sales revenues, or sometimes even negative sales revenues, representing a write-off or credit to departed customers.) The names of prospects and suspects may be in your database. "Guesstimates" by marketing and sales managers are the normal source for numbers of prospect and suspect information at the start-up.

Eric chose the standard customer segmentation: Top (1%), Big (4%), Medium (15%), and Small (80%). The black lines shown in Appendix A indicate where the customers are segmented. He discovered that the 450 Midwest region customers fell into segments with 4 in "Top," 18 in "Big," 68 in "Medium," and 360 in "Small," with revenue percentages of 28%, 23%, 27%, and 22% respectively, and sketched out a customer pyramid (see Figure II.3). That was the moment that Eric Dines decided to get moving with Customer Marketing—immediately.

Figure II.3

The InterTech Customer Pyramid

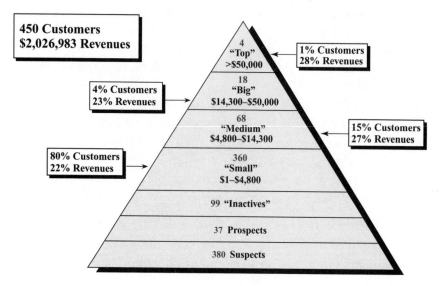

Keep Project Management Simple

Many people with big-company experience cringe at such terms as "Project Management Structure" or "Steering Committee." They recall endless meetings, exasperating power struggles, and nasty territorial disputes.

A Customer Marketing implementation project should be lean, mean, and simple, with the following elements.

Make the Management Team a Steering Committee.

Customer Marketing needs management commitment to make it work because the method involves the whole company or business unit. Thus it makes sense to put the implementation "in the line." But you don't have to create a new Steering Committee or some similar body to oversee the implementation process and resolve jurisdictional and territorial disputes. Simply add "Customer Marketing Progress Report" to the fixed agenda points of the Management Team meeting.

Select an optimal model project area.

If you are going to start with a model project, the number-one criterion for selecting the business unit or regions is that you have *the highest chance of success*. The last thing you need is to have the model project get into trouble because of organizational, personality, or business problems. So look for a business unit or region that is already successful and has strong management and enthusiastic employees. Consider that the people who participate in a successful model project will be the "evangelists" inspiring and helping other business units to implement later on.

Appoint a strong Project Manager.

The Project Manager is the leader of the implementation process. He or she must be a "make-it-happen" person with respect and authority. The Project Manager may be a member of the Management Team, a key manager of the model project business unit, or perhaps a bright, energetic young staff person.

Install a Customer Marketing Project Group.

The Customer Marketing Project Group is charged with timely and effective implementation of the method under the leadership of the Project Manager. Your Customer Marketing Project Group should include representatives from marketing, field sales, service, and IT, and other units with customer contact.

The InterTech Project Management Structure

Having made his first customer pyramid, Eric brought up the subject of Customer Marketing with his Management Team: Vincent Brown (production), Mary Palaglia (human resources), and Nils Novotny (finance and IT). (Eric considered himself marketing and sales manager.)

Eric proposed that the Midwest sales region be the site of a model project (surprise!). For one thing, the unit operated out of the headquarters building, meaning that the Management Team would be close to the action and could provide immediate support. And Bill de Vries, the regional sales manager, was a bright, enthusiastic young man who had the respect of the people working for him. He was the logical choice to be Project Manager.

The Management Team agreed with the model project proposal and welcomed the idea of serving as the Steering Committee.

In a later discussion with Bill de Vries, they agreed that the Project Team should consist of Bill, Alicia Potts (a bright young marketing trainee with excellent computer skills), and Fred Ramselaar.

$$\underline{\quad I.C. \quad}$$

Conduct a Parameters Workshop

Once you have your Project Team and structure in place, you should quickly bring your Management Team and Project Team together for a day to keep the momentum. The first half of the day should be dedicated to reach consensus on key issues. After lunch you need to determine what kinds of information you need to have on your customers and where you can find it.

Show and discuss the customer pyramid.

A picture is worth a thousand words. And there is nothing like a "real world" customer pyramid to explain the need for a Customer Relationship Management strategy.

Eric had refined the customer pyramid prior to the workshop, adding average revenue-per-customer data (see Figure II.4). It didn't take a rocket scientist to determine that InterTech was losing money on 80% of their customers, since their average revenue was only $1,244!

Specify your objectives.

What objectives do you want to achieve with Customer Marketing and Customer Relationship Management? Don't be tempted to set "soft" and unmeasurable goals such as "more understanding for the customer and his needs." Put some numbers on your goals, especially the three customer performance factors: customer value, customer behavior, and customer satisfaction.

Figure II.4

InterTech Customer Pyramid with Revenues

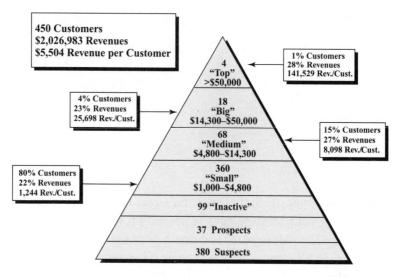

450 Customers
$2,026,983 Revenues
$5,504 Revenue per Customer

1% Customers
28% Revenues
141,529 Rev./Cust.

4
"Top"
>$50,000

4% Customers
23% Revenues
25,698 Rev./Cust.

18
"Big"
$14,300–$50,000

68
"Medium"
$4,800–$14,300

15% Customers
27% Revenues
8,098 Rev./Cust.

80% Customers
22% Revenues
1,244 Rev./Cust.

360
"Small"
$1,000–$4,800

99 "Inactive"

37 Prospects

380 Suspects

Eric Dines made quite clear the "official" InterTech objectives for Customer Marketing:

- *A 50% increase in operational profit, given a 3% increase in overhead, marketing, and sales and other fixed costs to match the expected inflation rate*
- *A 10% increase in sales revenues*
- *A "substantial" increase in customer satisfaction (difficult to quantify because InterTech had never really measured customer satisfaction in the past)*

Define your "value propositions."

To measure, manage, and improve customer satisfaction, you have to get an accurate reading on customer appreciation of your "value propositions," which your customers want and expect from you and your competitors (see Figure II.5). Value propositions can best be described in terms of "boxes," as described below:

- *"Box" value propositions* are the basic products (or services) you deliver to your customers, such as suits, temporary help workers, or fuel for your automobile.

Figure II.5

Identifying "Value Propositions"
(What do your customers want from you?)

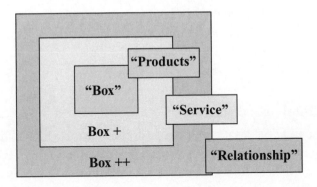

- *"Box +" value propositions* are the service aspects that accompany your basic product, such as tailoring the cuffs of the suit, handling the Social Security payments of the temporary help, and wiping the windows when you fill up a customer's tank.
- *"Box ++" value propositions* are those relationship aspects that make the customer very comfortable, happy, and ready to buy again, such as giving a free neck tie with a suit, having the temporary help secretary bring the customer a bunch of flowers on her first day, and—unasked—washing the car windows when you fill up at the gas pump.

The InterTech group spent a lot of time thinking about their value propositions. At the end of a (long!) morning, they reached concurrence on this list:

"Box" Value Propositions
- *Quality of construction*
- *Lifetime/durability/robustness*
- *Ease of installation*
- *Price/value for money*

"Box +" Value Propositions
- *Expertise of technical service*
- *Speed of technical service*
- *Delivery times*

"Box ++" Value Propositions
- *Understand customer's business*
- *Come up with ideas*
- *Complaint handling*
- *Availability of Account Manager*
- *Expertise of Account Manager*
- *Meet agreements and deadlines*
- *Telephone/correspondence is friendly*

Define Total Spend (factors).

Total Spend is the total amount a customer has or will spend on your category of products and services in a given period of time. For the supermarket owner, the food budget of the Simpson family is the Total Spend of that customer. What a company spends on airlines and hotels is the Total Spend of interest to the travel agent.

Total Spend is essential to know when setting goals and targets for the customer and deciding how much you are going to invest in getting a large share of it.

You have to define what Total Spend means for your company. A magazine selling advertisements can choose Total Spend to mean what a customer spends on other magazines or what the customer spends on all advertising, including radio and television.

Once you have defined Total Spend, your goal is to acquire or estimate the Total Spend numbers for each customer and prospect.

In some industries this is not difficult:

- If you know the store size and number of employees of an optician, you can estimate the total spend on prescription glasses within a bandwidth of 10% certainty.
- If you sell automobiles to fleet owners, the size and composition of a company's fleet of automobiles and trucks is public information. Since most fleet owners replace vehicles after three years, you only have to divide the fleet size by three to determine how many automobiles they are likely to buy next year.
- For consumer markets, if you know the number and ages of people in a family—and their zip code—you can figure out fairly accurately the amount of money that family will spend each year on groceries and clothing.

But in many cases the only way to find out the past and future Total Spend of customers and prospects is simply to ask them during a customer interview. (As a last resort, if you need some numbers but don't have time for interviews, you can ask your sales or services people for a "guesstimate.")

Finally, you need to identify some variables that will help you predict changes in a customer's Total Spend in the near future. For business-to-business customers this is often related to the industry and the size of the company. Market research and economic data are often useful for predicting the Total Spend of consumer segments.

The InterTech workshop members decided that the factors that would most affect the Total Spend of their customers and prospects were most likely to be

- *Customer plans and budgets*
- *The industry of the customer or prospect, namely:*
  - *Appliances*
  - *Machine tool suppliers*
  - *Others*
- *The size of the company, measured as number of employees*

Define Customer Share (factors).

Customer Share is the amount of purchasing a customer does with you as a percent of their Total Spend in your business category. Let's say you sell $100,000 of product in a year to both Customer A and Customer B. Customer A's Total Spend that year was $1,000,000; for Customer B it was $200,000. Thus your Customer Share for Customer A is 10%, and for Customer B it is 50%.

Once you know your share of a customer's Total Spend, you can start thinking about how to keep that share or increase it. What factors determine the share of the Total Spend you will get from your customers? Two factors are generally valid for every company:

- Customer satisfaction levels
- Strength of the competitors that are getting the share of customer that you are not

After some interesting debate and discussion, the InterTech work-
shop delegates agreed that these were key Customer Share factors
for their company:

- *Customer satisfaction scores*
- *Competitive strength as determined by the primary competitor*
- *The length of the customer relationship measured in years*
- *Customer Share of the previous year*

Conduct a Customer Information QuickScan.

Once you have defined Total Spend, Customer Share, and customer
satisfaction factors, you have to find out where you can get this critical
data, as well as the other information necessary for proper Customer
Relationship Management, such as:

- *Basic Information:* For starters, you need to know the name, address, telephone/fax numbers, and e-mail addresses of your customers and prospects.
- *"DMU" Information:* You also need to know who is on the "decision-making unit," namely, the buyer, the user, the final decision
  maker, and the influencers who will ultimately determine if, and
  how much, the customer will purchase from you.
- *Customer Financials:* To determine customer profitability, you will
  have to be able to identify costs that can be allocated to individual
  customers and prospects or segments thereof.
- *Customer Behavior Variables:* This is the measurement unit on
  which you will build your customer pyramid, usually sales revenues.

You will find it useful to make a Customer Information QuickScan
to guide your search for the information: where it is stored, in what
form, and how you can get it.

The results of the InterTech Customer Information QuickScan ex-
ercise conducted during the workshop provided a clear picture
of the needed information and its location. (see Figure II.6)
*   At the close of the workshop, Eric asked Bill to get the Project*

Figure II.6

Customer Information QuickScan

Information Requirement	Where Information Is Located			Data Format			How to Get Information
	Internal	Customer	3rd Party	Computer	Paper	In Heads	
Basic Information	Order Entry			X			Retrieve
"DMU" Information	Sales Dept.					X	Ask Sales
Customer Costs	Finance			X			Retrieve
Customer Behavior Variables							
* Order History (Products)	Order Entry			X			Retrieve
* Order History (Service)	Service			X			Retrieve
* Revenues	Finance			X			Retrieve
Total Spend Factors							
* Last Year Total Spend		X				X	Interview
* Industry Code			Credit Co.				Order
* Size of Company			Credit Co.				Order
"Customer Share Factors"							
* Last Year Customer Share	Finance			X			Calculate
* Competitive Supplier		X				X	Interview
* Satisfaction Levels		X				X	Interview
* Length of Relationship	Order Entry						Retrieve

Figure II.6 (continued)

Information Requirement	Where Information Is Located			Data Format			How to Get Information
	Internal	Customer	3rd Party	Computer	Paper	In Heads	
Value Propositions							
* "Box" Value Propositions							
—Quality of construction		X				X	Interview
—Lifetime/durability/robustness		X				X	Interview
—Ease of installation		X				X	Interview
—Range of products		X				X	Interview
* "Box+" Value Propositions							
—Expertise of technical service		X				X	Interview
—Speed of technical service		X				X	Interview
—Delivery times		X				X	Interview
* "Box++" Value Propositions							
—Understand customer's business		X				X	Interview
—Come up with ideas		X				X	Interview
—Complaint handling		X				X	Interview
—Availability of account manager		X				X	Interview
—Expertise of account manager		X				X	Interview
—Meet agreements and deadlines		X				X	Interview
—Telephone/correspondence is friendly		X				X	Interview

Group started on the diagnosis phase of Customer Marketing right away, beginning with the development of a questionnaire to capture the critical information stored in the heads of the InterTech customers.

Phase II: Diagnosis

Figure II.7

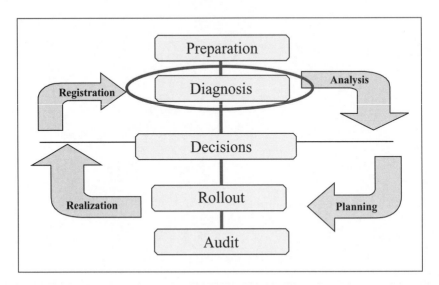

During the diagnosis phase of Customer Marketing, you will get and analyze information which will

- Provide you with new insights on the profitability, behavior and satisfaction of your customers—and how to improve these performance factors.
- Measure the degree of customer focus inside your company—and get valuable advice on how to increase it.
- Point the way towards a successful model project rollout and further implementation in the rest of your company.

Please note: the diagnostic phase activities are presented here in serial form. But you can perform a number of them at the same time.

Conduct Interviews with a Selection of Customers (and Prospects)

A Customer Marketing objective is to interview all your customers (and prospects). But at this preparation stage only a representative sample of customers will be interviewed so that you can

- Get an objective view of current customer satisfaction levels and identify improvement levels.
- Determine customer acceptance of the questionnaire so that you can make refinements in the rollout phase.
- Test the effectiveness of various methods for interviewing customers (face to face, by telephone, in writing, and via e-mail/Web site).
- Gather complete data on a selection of customers that you can use for training customer teams during the rollout phase.

Make a "customer selection."

Select a sample of 10% to 20% of the customers in your model project area representing customers from all layers of the pyramid. But you should hand-pick the top-tier customers who will be essentially "guinea pigs" for the interviews, choosing those whom you know will welcome the opportunity to help you test your questionnaire.

InterTech selected 50 customers and prospects to be subjected to the initial customer interviews. For reasons of space, we will in

Figure II.8

The InterTech Customer Selection

Customer Name	LY Pyramid	LY Revenue	Revenue per Cluster			
			Widgets	Plunkets	J-Bars	Whamos
Struckman	Top	$296,337	$ 8,606	$270,200	$17,247	$ 284
Boards Unlimited	Top	143,945	94,750	42,838	3,224	3,132
Silicon Sync	Big	42,365	34,038	4,105	3,097	1,125
Green Machine	Big	31,010	10,206	5,321	15,145	337
SpeedServ	Medium	13,659	10,842	910	1,549	358
Main	Medium	13,026	6,935	1,465	4,396	229
Sentinel Service	Medium	12,604	1,708	7,154	3,685	56
Colby Corp.	Small	4,791	2,736	1,198	766	90
Bates Milling	Small	1,717	1,662	0	0	55
Montpelier SA	Small	680	520	1	141	17
de Vries Inc.	Small	97	54	9	32	2
Bristol	Inactive	0	0	0	0	0
Wilkes Corp.	Inactive	0	0	0	0	0
Jones & Long	Prospect	0	0	0	0	0
British Techno	Prospect	0	0	0	0	0
Cellular Tel	Prospect	0	0	0	0	0
Bowdoin Bros.	Prospect	0	0	0	0	0

the remainder of this book work with 16 of the customer selection. In Figure II.8 they are listed by their "Last Year" (LY) pyramid position and revenue, split out by product cluster.

Construct your customer interview questionnaire.

The customer interview has as its key objective to learn everything you need to know about your customers to improve their profitability, behavior, and satisfaction while filling the gaps identified in the Customer Information QuickScan. Jan de Boer's method was very effective, but his method did not allow him to capture complete customer data: he was totally focused on upward migration in the pyramid. You want to know more. And if you want to know more, you have to use "funnel questioning": start with broad and general topics, then drill down to the specifics, such as

- Satisfaction levels with your core products and services
- Cross-selling and up-selling opportunities
- Discrepancies, or "gaps," between importance of a value proposition and satisfaction
- Loyalty indicators that ascertain if the customer
  - considers you the preferred supplier
  - is planning to buy from you next year
  - recommends you to colleagues, friends, and family
- Budgets for your product/service category in the future (Total Spend data)
- Identification of competitive suppliers (Customer Share data)
- Customer preferences for contact methods and frequencies
- Plus anything else you want to know from your customers but, until now, were afraid to ask!

Relying on her background and education in marketing research, Alicia Potts designed the customer interview questionnaire that can be found in Appendix B.

Interview the customer selection.

By interviewing the customer selection, you will get highly relevant information on these customers and prospects to measure customer satisfaction and get real-world data to improve their performance—and also to use when training customer teams in the rollout phase. These early customer interviews are also useful for testing and refining your questionnaire and the methods and media that are most appropriate for different customer types.

The Top and Big customers obviously require a face-to-face approach, starting with a "friendly," a customer who will be happy to be a test case for your customer interview. The Medium and promising Small customers can be handled with telephone interviews preceded by a letter alerting the customer of the interview. Try getting sufficient response from the remaining Small customers with a written—or e-mail—questionnaire (the offer of a small premium can raise response). Once you are confident that the questionnaire is acceptable and the methods/media effective, roll it out to the rest of the customer selection. (Note: Prior to conducting customer interviews by telephone—especially if you use a telemarketing agency—always send a letter explaining the objectives of the customer interview and informing the customer to expect the call.)

The InterTech "top dogs"—Eric Dines, Mike Shea, and Bill de Vries—each tried out a face-to-face customer interview. They were amazed to find that their customers responded warmly to the idea and were helpful in making adjustments to the questionnaire. Alicia Potts contracted with a local market research agency for the telephone and written interviews. The telephone interviews had a 73% completion rate, but the written questionnaires scored only a 20% response. They decided to scrap the written interviews, replacing them, in the future, with telephone interviews.

Diagnose the Value of Your Customers

While the customer interviews are taking place, you can go to work right away diagnosing customer value, or customer profitability. Your bookkeeping department and financial reports contain most of the information you need to start practicing Customer-Based Accounting, or CBA. (CBA is a customer-based version of Activity-Based Costing, or ABC!)

Controllers, administrators, and other financial people—not always champions of marketing and sales spending—often become enthusiastic about Customer-Based Accounting. You will start to hear things from them like "Finally, those guys in marketing are doing the right things!" As a result, the bookkeepers and controllers often provide enthusiastic help as you analyze, plan, and budget your marketing and sales activities.

Determine operational profit.

Operational profit is sometimes called "EBDIT," or earnings before depreciation, interest, and taxes. This number is a reflection of company performance based on transactions with customers.

> *Fred Ramselaar took on the task of diagnosing the value of InterTech's Midwest division customers. Using standard financial reports he readily identified the regional operational profit of $91,499, about 5% of revenues (see Figure II.9).*

Identify all your marketing and sales costs.

Marketing and sales costs normally take up the bulk of Customer Relationship Management spending and have a major impact on the prof-

Figure II.9

InterTech Operational Results

Revenues	$2,026,983	100%
Direct Costs	1,183,484	58%
Margin %	42%	
Margin	843,499	42%
General, Sales, Admin.	752,000	37%
Operational Profit	$91,499	5%

itability of a customer as revenue and margin per customer. Many companies calculate their marketing and sales costs at 5% to 10% of revenues. You may find during this exercise that your marketing and sales costs can be 20% or more because the CBA technique also includes marketing and sales overheads.

What are marketing and sales costs? You may find it useful to use these three cost clusters:

- *Sales costs* are those commercial costs incurred to influence the buying behavior of *individual customers*. Thus the salaries and expenses of the field sales force, telesales people, and (sometimes) service people are normally considered sales costs.
- *Marketing costs* are those commercial costs spent on activities to influence the buying behavior of customer groups rather than individual customers: direct mail, advertising, publicity, telemarketing campaigns, etc. Market research is another marketing cost to be considered.
- *Marketing and sales overheads* are indirect costs of the marketing and sales department: management salaries and fees, office space, automation, and other overheads used by or allocated to marketing and sales.

After deducting sales costs, marketing costs, and marketing and sales overheads from general sales and administrative costs, the remainder is pure overheads.

This exercise took Fred a bit more time to complete. But he was able to come up with the numbers shown in Figure II.10.

Figure II.10

Sales Costs	
Field Sales	$158,000
Internal Sales	100,000
Customer Service	25,000
Travel, Representation	19,000
Total Sales Costs	*$302,000*

Marketing Costs	
Advertising	$ 4,000
Mailings	3,000
Telemarketing	2,000
Exhibition	10,000
Representation	3,000
PR/Publicity	2,000
Customer Benefits	1,000
Total Marketing Costs	*$25,000*

M&S Overheads	
Sales Management	$25,000
Marketing Management	25,000
Automation	6,000
Office	4,000
Misc.	10,000
Total M&S Overheads	*$70,000*

General Overheads	
Office	$127,500
General Costs	170,000
Depreciation	43,000
Interest	14,500
Total Overheads	*$355,000*

Calculate your average per-customer revenue and profit and your marketing and sales ROI (return on investment).

- The *average turnover and profit per customer* is calculated by dividing revenue and profit by the number of (active) customers.
- The *average return on investment for marketing and sales* is calculated by dividing profit by all marketing and sales costs. The primary function of this ROI calculation is to provide a baseline measurement against which to judge improvements.

From the customer pyramid Fred knew that InterTech had 450 active customers last year. Making these calculations was a snap:

- *$4,505 revenue per customer*
- *$203 profit per customer*
- *23% ROI on marketing and sales*

Figure II.11

InterTech CustomerValue and ROI

Revenues	**$2,026,983**	**100%**
Direct Costs	**1,183,484**	**58%**
Margin %	42%	
Margin	**843,499**	**42%**
General Overheads	**355,000**	**18%**
Profit before M&S	**488,499**	**24%**
Marketing & Sales		
Sales Costs	302,000	15%
Marketing Costs	25,000	1%
M&S Overheads	70,000	3%
Total M&S Costs	**397,000**	**20%**
Operational Profit	**$91,499**	**5%**

Customers	*450*
Revenue per Customer	*$4,504*
Profit per Customer	*$203*
ROI on M&S	*23%*

Fred brought the numbers on his spreadsheet to his boss, Nils Novotny, and sent copies to Bill de Vries and Eric Dines. They were surprised that marketing and sales took up 20% of revenues. And they were curious about what the next steps would reveal concerning the profitability of customers by segment and individually.

Allocate margins and costs to customer pyramid segments.

This process can lead to some interesting discussions. For instance, bigger customers often get higher discounts, leading to lower margins. And how do you allocate overheads to customer segments: by revenues or number of customers? (Try allocating 50% of overheads by revenues and 50% by number of customers.) Allocation of marketing and sales costs per customer segments is also an issue: where in the customer pyramid do your salespeople spend what percentage of their time?

Remember, though, that Customer-Based Accounting does not need the same precision as a report for the shareholders, the Securities Exchange Commission, or the IRS. Your objective is to get a good understanding on what (kinds of) customers are profitable, which are not, and what you can do to raise customer profitability.

Fred, Nils, and Bill had a lively two-hour discussion allocating margins and costs to the different segments of the customer pyramid. At the end of the session, they had reached a consensus (See Figure II.12).

Analyze customer value per customer pyramid segment.

Having made the revenue, margin, and cost allocations per customer (segment), figuring out the profit and ROI per customer and/or customer segment is fairly routine with a spreadsheet.

Figure II.13 shows how Fred did it.

Calculate the profitability of individual customers.

You can then extrapolate the ratios of margins and costs per segment to individual customers to reach bottom line and ROI for each and every one of your customers. The results may surprise you!

Fred calculated the profitability of all the customers in the customer selection and showed the spreadsheet to Bill de Vries. Bill really couldn't believe the more than 2,000% ROI on large customers, but Fred's recalculation came up with the same results (see Figure II.14).

Try "What if?" scenarios with a planning matrix.

Once you have revenue and profit-per-customer numbers for each segment in your pyramid, you can execute "What if?" scenarios, such as:

"What if we migrate 5% of our customers up in the pyramid?"
"What if we lose two top customers?"

The possibilities are endless.

Figure II.12

InterTech Cost Allocation per Customer Segment

	Total	Top	Big	Medium	Small	Inactive	Prospects	Suspects
Noncustomers	*516*					*99*	*37*	*380*
Customers	*450*	*4*	*18*	*68*	*360*			
Revenues	$2,026,983	566,115	462,561	550,633	447,674			
Direct Costs	$1,183,484	339,529	276,039	322,228	245,688			
Margin	$843,499	226,586	186,522	228,405	201,987			
Margin %	42%	40%	40%	41%	45%			
General Overheads	$355,000	46,150	53,250	56,800	145,550	17,750	17,750	17,750
General Overheads %	100%	13%	15%	16%	41%	5%	5%	5%
Sales Costs	$302,000	15,100	30,200	75,500	120,800	15,100	30,200	15,100
Sales Costs %	100%	5%	10%	25%	40%	5%	10%	5%
Marketing Costs	$25,000	250	750	2,000	3,750	750	8,750	8,750
Marketing Costs %	100%	1%	3%	8%	15%	3%	35%	35%
M&S Overheads	$70,000	3,500	7,000	17,500	28,000	3,500	7,000	3,500
M&S Overheads %	100%	5%	10%	25%	40%	5%	10%	5%
Total M&S Costs	$397,000	18,850	37,950	95,000	152,550	19,350	45,950	27,350
Total M&S Costs %	100%	5%	10%	24%	38%	5%	12%	7%

Figure II.13

InterTech Customer Value Analysis per Pyramid Segment

Customers	Total	Top	Big	Medium	Small	Inactive	Prospects	Suspects
Number	450	4	18	68	360	99	37	380
Revenues	**$2,026,983**	**566,115**	**462,561**	**550,633**	**447,674**			
Production Costs	1,183,484	339,529	276,039	322,228	245,688			
Margin %	42%	40%	40%	41%	45%			
Margin	**843,499**	**226,586**	**186,522**	**228,405**	**201,987**			
Overheads	**355,000**	**46,150**	**53,250**	**56,800**	**145,550**	**17,750**	**17,750**	**17,750**
Result before M&S	**488,499**	**180,436**	**133,272**	**171,605**	**56,437**	**-17,750**	**-17,750**	**-17,750**
Sales Costs	302,000	15,100	30,200	75,500	120,800	15,100	30,200	15,100
Marketing Costs	25,000	250	750	2,000	3,750	750	8,750	8,750
M&S Overheads	70,000	3,500	7,000	17,500	28,000	3,500	7,000	3,500
Total M&S Costs	**397,000**	**18,850**	**37,950**	**95,000**	**152,550**	**19,350**	**45,950**	**27,350**
Operational Profit	**$91,499**	**161,586**	**95,322**	**76,605**	**-96,113**	**-37,100**	**-63,700**	**-45,100**
Analysis								
% Customers	100%	1%	4%	15%	80%	0%	0%	0%
% Revenues	100%	28%	23%	27%	22%	0%	0%	7%
% Marketing and Sales	100%	5%	10%	24%	38%	5%	12%	7%
% Profits	100%	177%	104%	84%	-105%	-41%	-70%	-49%
Revenue/Customer	$4,504	141,529	25,698	8,098	1,244	NA	NA	NA
Margin/Customer	1,874	56,646	10,362	3,359	561	NA	NA	NA
Overhead/Customer	789	11,538	2,958	835	404	179	480	47
Sales/Customer	671	3,775	1,678	1,110	336	153	816	40
Marketing/Customer	56	63	42	29	10	8	236	23
M&S Overhead/Customer	156	875	389	257	78	35	189	9
Marketing & Sales/Customer	882	4,713	2,108	1,397	424	195	1,242	72
Profit/Customer	203	40,396	5,296	1,127	-267	NA	NA	NA
M&S ROI	*23%*	*857%*	*251%*	*81%*	*-63%*	*NA*	*NA*	*NA*

Figure II.14

Customer Name	Last Year Pyramid	Last Year Revenues	Last Year Margin	General Overheads	Last Year Sales Costs	Last Year Mkt.Costs	Last Year M&S Overhead	Total M&S	Customer Profit	M&S ROI
Struckman	Top	$296,337	$118,535	$11,538	$3,775	$63	$875	$4,713	$102,285	2,170%
Boards Unlimited	Top	143,945	57,578	11,538	3,775	63	875	4,713	41,328	877%
Silicon Sync	Big	42,365	16,946	2,958	1,678	42	389	2,108	11,879	563%
Green Machine	Big	31,010	12,404	2,958	1,678	42	389	2,108	7,337	348%
SpeedServ	Medium	13,659	5,600	835	1,110	29	257	1,397	3,368	241%
Main	Medium	13,026	5,341	835	1,110	29	257	1,397	3,108	222%
Sentinel Service	Medium	12,604	5,168	835	1,110	29	257	1,397	2,935	210%
Colby Corp.	Small	4,791	2,156	404	336	10	78	424	1,328	313%
Bates Milling	Small	1,717	773	404	336	10	78	424	-55	-13%
Montpelier SA	Small	680	306	404	336	10	78	424	-522	-123%
de Vries Inc.	Small	97	44	404	336	10	78	424	-784	-185%
Bristol	Inactive	0		179	153	8	35	195	-375	-192%
Wilkes Corp.	Inactive	0		179	153	8	35	195	-375	-192%
Jones & Long	Prospect	0		480	816	236	189	1,242	-1,722	-139%
British Techno	Prospect	0		480	816	236	189	1,242	-1,722	-139%
Cellular Tel	Prospect	0		480	816	236	189	1,242	-1,722	-139%
Bowdoin Bros.	Prospect	0		480	816	236	189	1,242	-1,722	-139%

Figure II.15

"What if?" Scenario: Net Upward Migration of Six Customers

Pyramid Position	Last Year's Performance			Rev. per Customer	Profit per Customer
	Customers	Revenues	Profit		
Top	4	$566,115	$161,586	$141,529	$40,396
Big	18	462,561	95,322	25,698	5,296
Medium	68	550,633	76,605	8,098	1,127
Small	360	447,674	−96,113	1,244	−267
I/P/S			−145,900		
Totals	450	$2,026,983	$91,499	$4,504	$203

Pyramid Position	What if? Changes	What if? Performance		
		Customers	Revenue	Profit
Top	1	5	$707,643	$201,982
Big	2	20	513,957	105,913
Medium	3	71	574,926	79,985
Small	−6	354	440,213	−94,511
I/P/S				−145,900
Totals	0	450	$2,236,739	$147,469

Revenue Change		Profit Change	
$141,529	25%	$40,396	25%
51,396	11%	10,591	11%
24,293	4%	3,380	4%
−7,461	−2%	1,602	−2%
0		0	0%
$209,756	10%	$55,969	61%

Fred put together this "What if?" scenario spreadsheet and ran a simple simulation: "What if we had a net migration of six Small customers up the pyramid—three to Medium, two to Big, and one to Top—without raising fixed costs?"

The results: a 10% revenue increase and a whopping 61% boost in profits (see Figure II.15)

The potential CRM profit payoff for InterTech was there in black-and-white.

*Fred and Bill rushed the results into Eric, who studied the fig-
ures and asked rather laconically: "What happens if we lose just
one Top customer and one Big customer?"*

*In 10 seconds the spreadsheet told the story: the loss of one Top
and one Big customer would mean an 8% decline in revenues and
a 50% cut in profits (see Figure II.16)!*

Figure II.16

"What if?" Scenario: Loss of Top and Big Customers

Pyramid Position	Last Year's Performance			Rev. per Customer	Profit per Customer
	Customers	Revenues	Profit		
Top	4	$566,115	$161,586	$141,529	$40,396
Big	18	462,561	95,322	25,698	5,296
Medium	68	550,633	76,605	8,098	1,127
Small	360	447,674	−96,113	1,244	−267
I/P/S			−145,900		
Totals	450	$2,026,983	$91,499	$4,504	$203

Pyramid Position	What if? Changes	What if? Performance		
		Customers	Revenue	Profit
Top	−1	3	$424,586	$121,189
Big	−1	17	436,863	90,026
Medium	0	68	550,633	76,605
Small	0	360	447,674	−96,113
I/P/S				−145,900
Totals	−2	448	$1,859,757	$45,807

Revenue Change		Profit Change	
$−141,529	−25%	$−40,396	−25%
−25,698	−6%	−5,296	−6%
0	0%	0	0%
0	0%	0	0%
0		0	0%
$−167,226	−8%	$−45,692	−50%

*The flip side of CRM was also obvious. If you can't manage
the relationship with your key customers, you are going to be in
serious trouble.*

Figure II.17

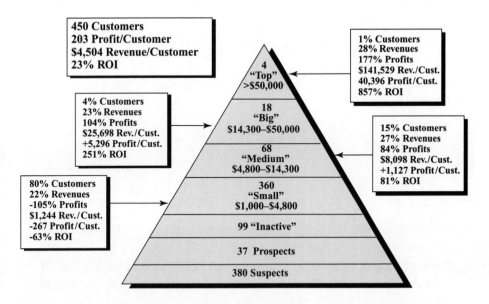

InterTech Pyramid: Customer-Based Accounting

450 Customers
203 Profit/Customer
$4,504 Revenue/Customer
23% ROI

1% Customers
28% Revenues
177% Profits
$141,529 Rev./Cust.
40,396 Profit/Cust.
857% ROI

4% Customers
23% Revenues
104% Profits
$25,698 Rev./Cust.
+5,296 Profit/Cust.
251% ROI

15% Customers
27% Revenues
84% Profits
$8,098 Rev./Cust.
+1,127 Profit/Cust.
81% ROI

80% Customers
22% Revenues
-105% Profits
$1,244 Rev./Cust.
-267 Profit/Cust.
-63% ROI

4 "Top" >$50,000

18 "Big" $14,300–$50,000

68 "Medium" $4,800–$14,300

360 "Small" $1,000–$4,800

99 "Inactive"

37 Prospects

380 Suspects

Make and distribute a customer pyramid with CBA results.

While spreadsheets are a great analytical tool, they are not often easy for everyone to understand. Make and disseminate your customer numbers to the Management Team and Project Group in the form of a customer pyramid that reflects the customer value in hard numbers.

Bill de Vries presented the InterTech customer pyramid (Figure II.17) and the "What if?" scenarios to the Management Team and the Project Group.
   The message was clear to everyone:

- *We are making good profits on the top 20% our customers.*
- *We are losing money on the rest of our customers.*
- *We should work hard at making some new large customers.*
- *We should review the money we are spending on small customers.*
- *We should move some of the small customers up the pyramid!*

Diagnose the Behavior of
Your Customers

In this phase you will link actual customer behavior and the information on factors that affect that behavior. By doing so, you can calculate the potential of individual customers and prospects. The analysis of customer behavior will be critical for your setting specific goals and making account plans to reach those goals.

Combine customer interview data with the other QuickScan information.

The output from the customer interviews and the follow-up from the Customer Information QuickScan will result in a wealth of information on your customers and prospects—starting the customer selection for the pilot project. This information is, of course, crucial for Customer Relationship Management.

You may have a sophisticated customer database in house, a simple contact manager, or perhaps just a spreadsheet. No matter which system you use, it is essential to link all relevant information—especially Total Spend and Customer Share (factors)—to each customer.

Alicia Potts took charge of this step at InterTech (see Figure II.18). She was able to get the information on Total Spend by reviewing the customer interviews and the Total Spend factors by buying the information from their credit check agency, which also sold this data to direct marketers:

Figure II.18

InterTech Total Spend Factors

Customer Name	Last Year Total Spend	Number of Employees	Customer Industry
Struckman	$592,700	>1,000	M-Tools
Boards Unlimited	202,700	500–999	Appliance
Silicon Sync	529,600	500–999	Appliance
Green Machine	34,800	250–499	M-Tools
SpeedServ	151,800	250–499	Other
Main	13,000	>1,000	M-Tools
Sentinel Service	18,300	500–999	Appliance
Colby Corp.	110,000	100–249	Appliance
Bates Milling	18,900	100–249	Other
Montpelier SA	7,000	100–249	Other
de Vries Inc.	4,600	500–999	Other
Bristol	58,000	500–999	Other
Wilkes Corp.	45,000	250–499	M-Tools
Jones & Long	158,000	>1,000	Appliance
British Techno	43,000	250–499	Appliance
Cellular Tel	12,000	<100	Other
Bowdoin Bros.	3,900	500–999	Other

- *The size of a customer, coded by number of employees*
- *The industry of a customer, listed by the first number of the SIC code*

With the Total Spend data on hand, Alice was able to calculate the Customer Share of the customers in the customer selection (see Figure II.19). You will discover in the next section how InterTech made further use of the information on the customer share factors:

- *Customer satisfaction*
- *The primary competitor fighting against InterTech for the business*
- *The longevity of the relationship with each customer*

Figure II.19

InterTech Customer Share and Customer Share Factors

Customer Name	Last Year Total Spend	Last Year Revenue	Last Year Share of Customer	Customer Satisfaction	Main Competition	Length of Relationship
Struckman	$592,700	$296,337	50%	4.2	Smit	>10 years
Boards Unlimited	202,700	143,945	71%	3.7	WidgFlex	3–5 years
Silicon Sync	529,600	42,365	8%	2.2	Delta	6–10 years
Green Machine	34,800	31,010	89%	3.3	Other	>10 years
SpeedServ	151,800	13,659	9%	3.8	Delta	< 1 year
Main	13,000	13,026	100%	2.7	Sole Supp	3–5 years
Sentinel Service	18,300	12,604	69%	3.7	Delta	>10 years
Colby Corp.	110,000	4,791	4%	3.5	Delta	2–5 years
Bates Milling	18,900	1,717	9%	3.0	Smit	1–2 years
Montpelier SA	7,000	680	10%	3.2	WidgFlex	3–5 years
de Vries Inc.	4,600	97	2%	4.0	Other	>10 years
Bristol	58,000	0			Other	< 1 year
Wilkes Corp.	45,000	0			Delta	6–10 years
Jones & Long	158,000	0			Other	0 years
British Techno	43,000	0			Smit	0 years
Cellular Tel	12,000	0			Delta	0 years
Bowdoin Bros.	3,900	0			WidgFlex	0 years

Although the volume of data at this stage of the diagnosis may not be reliable for sophisticated statistical analyses like regression analysis, you won't need to be a rocket scientist to detect some collations and patterns.

For Alicia Potts and her InterTech colleagues, some patterns were becoming clear. They came up with these conclusions:

- *Big companies spend more than small companies (no surprise!).*
- *Appliance and machine tool total spending are about the same.*
- *High Customer Share is related to high customer satisfaction.*

- *Low Customer Share is related to the presence of competitor Delta on site.*

Make a historical migration matrix.

While your customer pyramids and the "flat file database" are often revealing, they are only a "snapshot" of your customers at a specific point in time. You will also want to know the dynamics of what happened—and what can happen—in your customer pyramid. How many customers went up the pyramid last year? How many went down? How many customers did you win? How many did you lose? You can get these answers in a historical migration matrix.

A historical migration matrix gives you a dynamic view of customer behavior in a period of time. A historical migration matrix reveals which and how many of your customers in a given period of time

- Stayed in their customer pyramid level.
- Upgraded to a higher level in the pyramid.
- Dropped to inactive status.
- Revived from inactive to active status.
- Were converted to customer status from prospect status.

This information from the historical migration matrix gives you insights on customer mobility in the past, thereby helping you make realistic plans for customer mobility in the future.

In addition, detailed analysis of the customers that go up, stay the same, or go down in the customer pyramid can reveal characteristics that may be used to refine and validate Total Spend and Customer Share factors. To make a migration matrix, you need, of course, customer behavior data on two or more time periods.

Alicia had revenue data on InterTech customers for last year ("Last Year") and the year before last ("YBL"). Using this data, she made a historical migration matrix for InterTech (see Figure II.20).

The axis on the left (YBL) shows how many of what kind of customers were in the pyramid at the end of the year before last. To the right shows the behavior of those customers during last year.

Figure II.20

InterTech Migration Matrix

	"YBL"	Top	Big	Medium	Small	Inactive	Prospects	Suspects
Top	3	*2*	*0*	*1*	*0*	*0*	*0*	*0*
Big	16	*1*	*8*	*3*	*2*	*2*	*0*	*0*
Medium	61	*1*	*5*	*37*	*16*	*2*	*0*	*0*
Small	375	*0*	*2*	*22*	*312*	*39*	*0*	*0*
Inactive	64	*0*	*2*	*1*	*5*	*56*	*0*	*0*
Prospects	37	*0*	*1*	*4*	*8*	*0*	*24*	*0*
Suspects	410	*0*	*0*	*0*	*17*	*0*	*13*	*380*
"Last Year"	*450*	*4*	*18*	*68*	*360*			
						99	37	380

For instance, of the three Top customers from YBL, two stayed in the Top level, but one dropped to the Medium level. Of the 16 Big customers, only 8 stayed at the Big level; 1 migrated up to Top level, 3 downgraded to Medium level, 2 to Small, and 2 became inactive. And so forth.

At the bottom of the pyramid, you can see the net result of changes per pyramid segment. There were 4 Top customers at the end of last year vs. 3 the year before last; 18 Big customers vs. 16 last year; 68 Medium customers vs. 61 last year; and 360 Small customers vs. 375 last year.

Check your customer statistics.

The migration matrix provides you with insights on the mobility of your customers up, down, in, and out of the customer pyramid. These are useful in helping you make realistic customer plans and for benchmarking between planning periods and among business units.

The migration matrix revealed the InterTech customer statistics shown in Figure II.21.

Verify the feasibility of your "What if?" scenarios.

You can also project your customer migration pattern of last year on to the next year to see if your "What if?" scenarios are realistic—or to develop one.

Figure II.21

Summary of Last Year Customer Movement

Behavior	Number	Percentage
Ugraded	31	7%
Kept	359	79%
Downgraded	22	5%
Lost	43	9%
Reactivated	8	2%
Created	30	7%
Identified	13	3%
Total Active	*450*	*100%*

Alicia projected the migration patterns of the previous year on the current customer pyramid, which revealed a net upward migration of eight customers (see Figure II.22).

She then plugged these customer migration numbers into the "What if?" scenario spreadsheet. The bottom-line results were quite similar to Eric's projection: a 12% increase in revenues and a 69% profit hike (see Figure II.23).

Eric was pleased to see these scenarios and numbers from his staff. But he was well aware that customers are likely to migrate

Figure II.22

Customer Migration Projection: Next Year

	Last Year	Top	Big	Medium	Small	Inactive	Prospects	Suspects
Top	4	3	0	1	0	0	0	0
Big	18	1	9	3	2	2	0	0
Medium	68	1	6	41	18	2	0	0
Small	360	0	2	21	300	37	0	0
Inactive	99	0	3	2	8	87	0	0
Prospects	37	0	1	4	8	0	24	0
Suspects	380	0	0	0	16	0	12	352
Customers Next Year	450	5	21	72	352			
Change	0	1	3	4	–8	128	36	352

Figure II.23

Pyramid Position	Last Year's Performance			Revenue per Customer	Profit per Customer
	Customers	Revenues	Profit		
Top	4	$566,115	$161,586	$141,529	$40,396
Big	18	462,561	95,322	25,698	5,296
Medium	68	550,633	76,605	8,098	1,127
Small	360	447,674	−96,113	1,244	−267
I/P/S			−145,900		
Totals	450	$2,026,983	$91,499	$4,504	$203

Pyramid Position	What if? Changes	What if? Performance		
		Customers	$ Revenue	$ Profit
Top	1	5	707,643	201,982
Big	3	21	539,654	111,209
Medium	4	72	583,023	81,111
Small	−8	352	437,726	−93,977
I/P/S				−145,900
Totals	0	450	$2,268,047	$154,425

Revenue Change		Profit Change	
$141,529	25%	40,396	25%
77,093	17%	15,887	17%
32,390	6%	4,506	6%
−9,948	−2%	2,136	−2%
0		0	0%
$241,064	12%	$62,925	69%

upward only if they are satisfied—in fact, very satisfied—with InterTech products and services.

He called in Bill de Vries for a status report on the customer
satisfaction diagnosis.

Diagnose the Satisfaction of
Your Customers

Most companies that measure customer satisfaction get a written report with texts, charts, and tables. The report contains valuable feedback from a statistically reliable sample of customers who have
provided their opinions on an anonymous basis. With this information in hand, the company can make improvements in products, services, and customer relationship processes, track trends, compare
differences between business units, and so on.

Measuring customer satisfaction using the Customer Marketing
"customer interview" also provides you with information to improve
your products, services, and customer relationship processes. But
there are some major differences in the way the customer feedback is
captured.

- Customers give their opinions and satisfaction scores openly, not
  on an anonymous basis.
- The interviewer may be an employee of the company—and in face-
  to-face interviews probably has an existing relationship with the interviewee!

Scientifically correct researchers will protest that customer satisfaction data from the customer interview method may fall short on
precision and statistical reliability. And they are absolutely correct.
Thus you may want to conduct a more classical and anonymous cus-

tomer satisfaction survey parallel to the customer interview program.

But in our experience, the feedback from your customer interviews will be loud and clear about what you are doing right and what you are doing wrong. After all, the objective is not to have a nice report but to measure satisfaction levels and then make improvements. Plus you will get these advantages from the customer interviews:

- You will learn which customers are unhappy and can immediately start solving their problems.
- You will learn which customers are happy and can immediately start getting more of their business.
- You will learn which customers do not know your full range of products and services and can immediately start educating them.
- Your employees who conduct customer interviews will become highly sensitized to the need for customer care.
- Your customer interviews will probably pay for themselves immediately because they tend to generate unexpected orders and/or an interview may stop the defection of a dissatisfied customer whose problem could be fixed on the spot by the interviewer.

You can diagnose customer satisfaction scores two ways:

- *Aggregated scores* to identify aspects of your business that customers agree you need to improve.
- *Individual scores* to identify ways to increase the satisfaction of customers with high (potential) profitability.

Analyze aggregated scores: core product satisfaction

The first thing you want to see is how you are doing with your core products. What are satisfaction levels compared to what is optimal? What is the ratio of "highly satisfied" vs. "satisfied"—and lower?

Eric Dines was pleased to see that a large majority of his customers were highly satisfied or satisfied with the product (see Figure II.24). But he vowed to get the number of highly satisfied customers above 50%.

Figure II.24

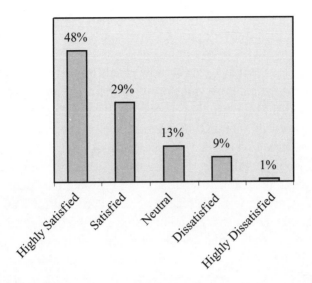

The way to improve product satisfaction became evident when he saw the per-product scores versus the optimum of 5.0 and compared with InterTech totals for all products (see Figure II.25). The Johnson Bars were pulling down the scores. He made a note to call the manufacturer.

Figure II.25

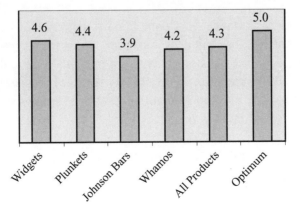

Analyze aggregated scores: value propositions

You need to know how customers rate your performance in delivering the value propositions for your products, service, and relationship. This is what customer satisfaction measurement is all about.

But it is also essential to know how much importance your customers place on each of your value propositions. You may be spending lots of money on fancy brochures, but customers don't value them highly—or even read them. On the other hand, you may think a four-hour response time to a service call is very good, but your customers want that time cut in half.

Finally, you may be able to segment your customers by their needs, as expressed in the importance placed on value propositions, and treat them accordingly. For instance, you may find a group of "Commodity" buyers who think only price and don't want service. Or a group of "Take care of me!" buyers who want lots of service and are less interested in price.

Thus, in diagnosing your aggregated scores for value propositions, you want to look at satisfaction scores vs. importance scores and the size of the "gap" that separates them.

The untiring Alicia Potts produced a spreadsheet to report on customer scoring of InterTech's value propositions, which she showed to Bill de Vries first as the man responsible for the satisfaction of these customers (see Figure II.26).

Alicia also gave him a chart that made the "gaps" quite visible (see Figure II.27).

With your importance vs. satisfaction scores, you can make a "Priority Action List" that balances customer scores for importance of a value proposition vs. customer satisfaction with your ability to deliver that value proposition. The Priority Action List segments your value propositions into four categories, each with its own message for the value proposition in that category:

- High Importance (>4.0) and Low Satisfaction (<4.0): *Fix these NOW!*
- High Importance (>4.0) and High Satisfaction (>4.0): *Keep up the good work!*

Figure II.26

InterTech Value Propositions: Importance vs. Satisfaction

"Box" Value Propositions	Satisfaction	Importance	Gap
— Quality of construction	4.2	4.5	0.3
— Lifetime/durability/robustness	4.1	4.6	0.5
— Ease of installation	3.9	4.4	0.5
— Price/value for money	3.8	4.8	1.0
Product Summary	**4.0**	**4.6**	**0.6**
* "Box +" Value Propositions	Satisfaction	Importance	Gap
— Expertise of technical service	4.0	4.6	0.6
— Speed of technical service	3.9	4.5	0.6
— Delivery times	3.3	4.3	1.0
Service Summary	**3.7**	**4.5**	**0.7**
* "Box ++" Value Propositions	Satisfaction	Importance	Gap
— Understand customer's business	4.1	4.9	0.8
— Come up with ideas	4.1	4.3	0.2
— Complaint handling	3.7	4.2	0.5
— Availability of account manager	4.1	4.3	0.2
— Expertise of account manager	3.9	4.4	0.5
— Meet agreements and deadlines	3.9	4.6	0.7
— Telephone/correspondence is friendly	4.1	4.0	-0.1
Relationship Summary	**4.0**	**4.4**	**0.4**
InterTech Total	**3.9**	**4.5**	**0.6**

- Low Importance (<4.0) and (<4.0) Low Satisfaction: *Fix these when you have time!*
- Low Importance (<4.0) and High Satisfaction (>4.0): *Applause— but is it worth it?*

The gap scores can also indicate need for attention, even if the satisfaction score is not so bad (See Figure II.28).

It didn't take Bill much time to see that a cluster of complaints— speed, delivery times, meeting agreements—was a clear signal

Figure II.27

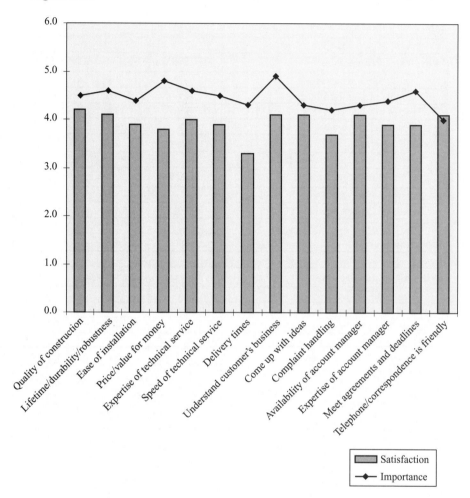

that while his team might be good salespeople, they were having problems delivering what they sold! InterTech's "back office" needed looking at. (Eric recognized the "Value for Money" scores as a reaction to a new discount policy.)

Analyze aggregated scores: loyalty indicators

What is the relationship between customer satisfaction and customer loyalty? As discussed earlier, reasonably satisfied customers defect.

Figure II.28

Area	Value Proposition	Satisfaction	Importance	Action
Service	*Delivery times*	*3.3*	*4.3*	*Fix Now!*
Product	*Price/value for money*	*3.8*	*4.8*	*Fix Now!*
Relation	*Meet agreements and deadlines*	*3.9*	*4.6*	*Fix Now!*
Service	*Speed of technical service*	*3.9*	*4.5*	*Fix Now!*
Service	Expertise of technical service	4.0	4.6	Keep it up!
Relation	Expertise of account manager	4.1	4.4	Keep it up!
Relation	Complaint handling	4.1	4.2	Keep it up!
Relation	Understand customer's business	4.1	4.9	Keep it up!
Product	Lifetime/durability/robustness	4.1	4.6	Keep it up!
Relation	Availability of account manager	4.1	4.3	Keep it up!
Product	Ease of installation	4.2	4.4	Keep it up!
Product	Quality of construction	4.2	4.5	Keep it up!
Relation	Come up with ideas	3.7	3.8	Fix Later!
Relation	*Telephone/correspondence is friendly*	*4.1*	*3.7*	*Great!*

You can sometimes identify possible defectors by posing some questions that will provide loyalty indicators:

1. To what degree are we a preferred supplier?
2. Do you think we will be doing business together 12 to 24 months from now?
3. Do you/would you recommend our company to others?

The reactions of customers when the questions are put to them—and the discussion that quite often takes place—are much more important than the statistics. But the statistics are useful to store up to see if there are changes at the next measurement.

Figures II.29–31 show how InterTech scored on the loyalty indicators.

How would you describe our supplier status for our range of products and services?

Figure II.29

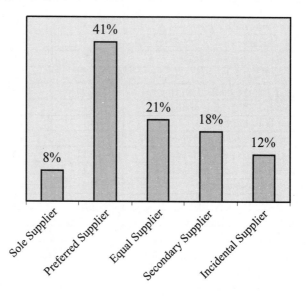

Do you expect that we will continue doing business with each other in the coming 12 to 24 months?

Figure II.30

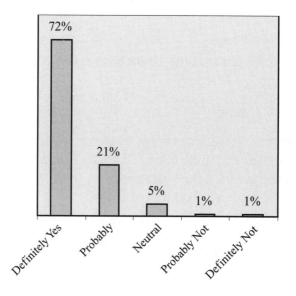

Do you/would you recommend InterTech to others?

Figure II.31

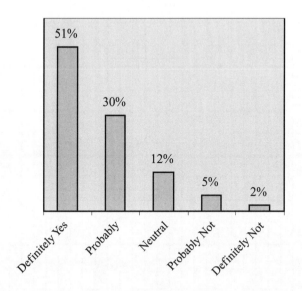

51%

30%

12%

5%

2%

Definitely Yes   Probably   Neutral   Probably Not   Definitely Not

Analyze individual customer scores.

The aggregate scores are necessary to identify areas where the experts—your customers—agree that improvements are needed over a period of time.

The satisfaction scores on a customer level can save or make you money immediately.

- You can contact dissatisfied customers immediately to resolve their problems and possibly prevent their defection.
- You can contact very satisfied customers with a low Customer Share and invite them to move up the customer pyramid.
- You can contact very satisfied customers with a high Customer Share and invite them to provide references.

Bill de Vries saw immediately that there were some unhappy campers in the customer selection (see Figure II.32). Silicon Sync obviously had a service problem. And while the people at Main were happy with the products, there was something wrong in the

Figure II.32

InterTech Customer Satisfaction Scores at the Customer Level (Summary)

Customer Name	Product (Box)		Service (Box +)		Relationship (Box ++)		Preferred Supplier	Will Continue	Reference	Overall Score
	Import.	Satis.	Import.	Satis.	Import.	Satis.				
Struckman	5	5	4	4	4	3	4	5	5	4
Boards Unlimited	5	3	4	4	5	4	4	4	4	3
Silicon Sync	4	3	4	1	4	2	3	3	2	2
Green Machine	5	3	5	3	5	3	3	5	4	4
SpeedServ	5	4	5	4	4	4	3	5	4	4
Main	4	3	4	3	5	3	2	3	2	3
Sentinel Service	4	4	5	3	4	3	3	4	5	4
Colby Corp.	5	4	4	3	5	3	3	5	4	4
Bates Milling	4	3	4	3	5	3	3	2	4	2
Montpelier SA	4	4	5	3	4	2	3	3	4	3
de Vries Inc.	4	4	5	4	3	4	4	4	4	4
Bristol										
Wilkes Corp.										
Jones & Long										
British Techno										
Cellular Tel										
Bowdoin Bros.										
Total	*4.5*	*3.6*	*4.5*	*3.2*	*4.4*	*3.1*	*3.2*	*3.9*	*3.8*	*3.4*

relationship. He called both companies immediately to make an appointment to remedy the situation.

On the other hand, he saw that Bob Struckman, one of his major customers, appeared to be a happy camper and invited him to lunch.

II.E.

Diagnose Your Customer Focus

We have discussed how IT and statistical tools can help you measure customer profitability, behavior, and satisfaction. But how can you put numbers against "soft stuff" such as customer focus?

It's really quite simple: you ask the experts to score your customer focus.

No, we don't mean the black-suited consultants, but the men and women on the work floor who are dealing with customers every day, know their complaints, know how it can be done better.

Figure II.33

How Can You Measure Customer Focus?

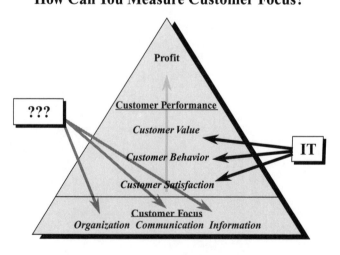

Undertake a Customer Focus Self-Assessment.

All you have to do is ask all your managers and staff to complete the "Customer Focus Self-Assessment" form and you will get a very clear idea where you need to get busy making improvements (see Figure II. 34).

As you can see, they will score 18 items that answer two questions:

- What is the status of that item in your company today?
- What priority should be given to improving the item?

The tool should be used anonymously. But you can use a "tick box" too so that the users can identify themselves as managers vs. staff or working in department X, Y, or Z. You can then make comparisons or do some internal benchmarking.

Give it a try now—it takes only about five minutes!

Eric Dines continued a tradition started by his father—the quarterly "AHOB Meeting" (AHOB stands for All Hands on Board)—during which the quarterly results and important news were shared with all managers and staff. Sometimes an outside speaker was also invited to provide insights or ideas on interesting topics.

Eric used the AHOB to ask his managers and staff to complete the Customer Focus Self-Assessment form. He promised to present the results at the following AHOB meeting.

After the meeting Eric asked Fred Ramselaar to do the spreadsheet work on this project. (Alicia Potts was taking a hard-earned vacation to recover from the customer interview/satisfaction project.)

Since Fred had seen how Alicia made a gap chart for the customer satisfaction survey, he used the same technique to dramatize the gaps between the situation and priority scores for the 18 customer focus issues (see Figure II.35).

Figure II.34

	Customer Focus Self-Assessment
	Use this tool to assess how your company deals with your customers. Give each statement two scores from 1 to 5.
	Situation Score: What is the situation on this issue in our company today? (5 = excellent, 4 = good, 3 = neutral, 2 = poor, 1 = bad)
	Priority Score: What priority should this issue have in our company? (5 = very high, 4 = high, 3 = neutral, 2 = low, 1 = none)

		Situation	Priority
1. Management	Management is committed to improving the customer focus of our company.		
2. Management	Management sets an example for customer focus by their own actions.		
3. Management	Management provides a sufficient budget (especially in time) to improve customer focus.		
4. Employees	Our employees have sufficient know-how and experience to deal with customers properly.		
5. Employees	The customer's needs are central in the thoughts and actions of our employees.		
6. Employees	Departments with customer contact work together as teams.		
7. Methods and Media	We use the most effective methods and media to accomplish goals at the lowest cost.		
8. Methods and Media	Our communications with customers demonstrate that we know them and their needs.		
9. Methods and Media	Our customer communications stress the benefits of our products and services rather than describing their features.		
10. Contact - Logistics	A contact and communication plan is made for every customer.		
11. Contact - Logistics	The execution of customer contacts is registered in procedures and diaries.		
12. Contact - Logistics	Noncommercial communication (correspondence, invoices, etc.) is "customer friendly."		
13. Customer Information	We have information that is useful to determine customer potential and to communicate with the right customer, about the right product, at the right time.		
14. Customer Information	Our customer information is complete.		
15. Customer Information	Our customer information is up-to-date.		
16. System	Our CIS* makes it easy to analyze customers and communicate with them via mail, telephone and face-to-face.		
17. System	Our CIS* is flexible (easy to make changes to meet our needs).		
18. System	Our CIS* can make available information about customers to anyone who needs it.		

* Customer Information System.

Figure II.35

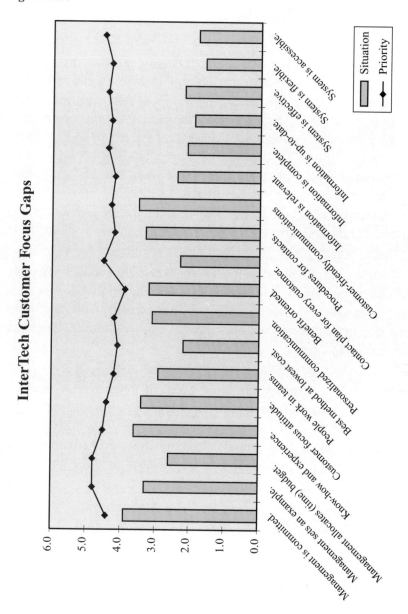

InterTech Customer Focus Gaps

Analyze your customer focus scores and gaps to identify improvement priorities.

The InterTech customer focus scores and gap patterns are very representative of what we have seen in thousands of self-assessment forms in more than 10 years:

- Managers assess their customer focus higher than the staff but admit that they do not devote enough time to the process. (Employees, on the other hand, tend to assess their customer focus higher than managers, expressing doubt about management commitment and contradicting management's claim to set a good example.)
- Customer contact planning always produces a big gap—people see that it is important but is not often done.
- The lowest situation scores and highest gaps are inevitably allocated to the six items on customer information and systems.

Looking at the self-assessment scores can help you identify priorities for improvement. More often than not, the priority scores come out higher than 4.0, since everyone would like to see all the items mentioned in perfect condition. Thus you have to look more to the situation scores and gaps.

- The highest priority should be given to items with a situation score less than 3.0, since this is a clear signal that something is wrong.
- You should then turn your attention to items with a situation score of 3.0 or higher, which have a higher than average gap for all items.

Eric Dines saw immediately that a major improvement effort was needed in the customer information and systems area. There were also clear signals from his managers and staff that some aspects of teamwork and customer planning needed looking at. Finally, Eric was a bit chagrined to discover that his people didn't think that "management" was spending enough time on improving customer focus.

Figure II.36

Domain	Item	Situation	Priority	"Gap"	
Org—Mgt	Management is committed.	3.9	4.4	0.5	
Org—Mgt	Management sets an example.	3.3	4.8	1.5	
Org—Mgt	Management allocates (time) budget.	2.6	4.8	2.2	Priority
Management		**3.3**	**4.7**	**1.4**	
Org—Staff	Know-how and experience.	3.6	4.5	0.9	
Org—Staff	Customer focus attitude.	3.4	4.4	1.0	
Org—Staff	People work in teams.	2.9	4.2	1.3	Priority
Staff		**3.3**	**4.4**	**1.1**	
Com—MMM	Best method at lowest cost.	2.2	4.1	1.9	Priority
Com—MMM	Personalized communication.	3.1	4.2	1.1	
Com—MMM	Benefit oriented.	3.2	3.9	0.7	
Message/Method/Media		**2.8**	**4.1**	**1.2**	
Com—Log	Contact plan for every customer.	2.3	4.5	2.2	Priority
Com—Log	Procedures for contacts.	3.3	4.2	0.9	
Com—Log	Customer-friendly communications.	3.5	4.3	0.8	
Contact Logistics		**3.0**	**4.3**	**1.3**	
Info—Cus Info	Information is relevant.	2.4	4.2	1.8	Priority
Info—Cus Info	Information is complete.	2.1	4.4	2.3	Priority
Info—Cus Info	Information is up-to-date.	1.9	4.3	2.4	Priority
Customer Info		**2.1**	**4.3**	**2.2**	Priority
Info—Systems	System is effective.	2.2	4.4	2.2	Priority
Info—Systems	System is flexible.	1.6	4.3	2.7	Priority
Info—Systems	System is accessible.	1.8	4.5	2.7	Priority
Customer Info Systems		**1.9**	**4.4**	**2.5**	Priority
Totals		**2.7**	**4.4**	**1.6**	

Eric told his secretary to cancel all appointments on the following day.

It was high time to evaluate all the output from the Customer Marketing diagnosis and decide where to go from there.

Phase III: Decisions

Figure II.37

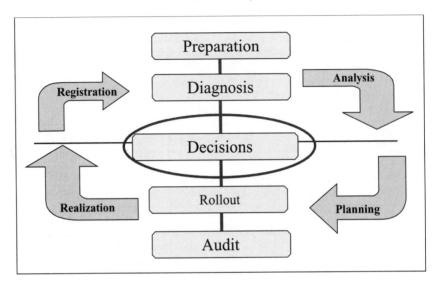

When you have completed your Customer Marketing diagnosis, you will have information and output that allows you to move on to the decision-making phase (see Figure II.37).

Set up a customer "scorecard."

You will have in hand data to make for yourself a "scorecard" with key customer performance and customer focus numbers against which you can measure improvements and benchmark against business units or other companies.

Get CRM advice from the experts.

The real experts on Customer Relationship Management—your customers and your people who deal with them—have provided you a wealth of information, advice, and suggestions about what needs to be done to improve customer satisfaction, behavior, and profitability.

Make "go/no go" decisions.

The Customer Marketing diagnosis process does not have much impact on anyone other than the project team members. But the rollout can involve everyone in the company with improvement activities for customer satisfaction and customer focus. And the managers and staff put into customer teams will be confronted with change.

Thus, if you give the "go" decision, you are committed to changing and improving the ways you deal with your customers. And if you have any experience with implementing TQM or similar programs, then you know that changing and improving the way people work takes time, effort, patience, and persistence.

There are two questions that you need to ask yourself in making the "go/no go" decision:

1. *To what extent will the implementation of CRM with the Customer Marketing method contribute to meeting or exceeding our business objectives?*
   Will implementation really help you make your numbers next year or the year thereafter? Will implementation help you fend off the competition? If the answer is yes, then go for it. But before you make the decision, answer the next question.

2. *What is the likelihood that implementation of CRM with the Customer Marketing method will be a success?*
   We have learned the hard way that there are circumstances that make the successful implementation of Customer Marketing very difficult. If you have encountered one or more of these situations during the diagnosis, think carefully about postponing your roll-out.

   – *Extreme customer dissatisfaction* with your products, services, and relationships. You must remedy these issues before raising customer expectations.
   – *A major reorganization* will soon be announced or started. You can't implement anything in the midst of turmoil. (Note: Customer Marketing implementation can work well when the reorganization dust is settling down—people are generally happier when turning away from internal battles to think about pyramids about customers.)
   – *Serious financial difficulty.* It is very difficult for managers and staff to "think customer" if they fear the company may soon go belly up.

Once you have made the rollout phase "Go" decision, then you and the management team/project team need to:

- Decide for which customer satisfaction and customer focus issues improvement groups should be installed.
- Decide how, when, and where to organize the key activities of the rollout phase:
  - Customer Marketing Kick-off
  - Customer-Based Business Planning Workshop
  - Customer Team Workshops

Let's see what the people at InterTech did—and decided.

Eric Dines himself spent a day reviewing all the diagnosis output and patched together the first "InterTech Customer Scorecard," as shown in Figure II.38. As you will see, he included all the key Customer Marketing metrics and added the specific areas to be improved:

Customer Performance Metrics	Customer Focus Metrics
Profit per customer	*Organization scores (summary)*
Revenue per customer	*Communication scores (summary)*
Customer satisfaction/ loyalty scores	*Information scores (summary)*
Improvement item	*Priority items*

While looking at the numbers, he recalled his "What if?" simulation showing a profit increase of 69% if customer migration patterns of last year repeated this year. Surely some major profit increases could be realized by implementing CRM with Customer Marketing. And the diagnosis had not uncovered any severe customer satisfaction or customer focus problems that would harm the chances of a rollout.

But Eric, who knows the value of "bottom up," called in Bill de Vries to look at the scorecard and offer his views on the "go/no go" decision. Of course, Bill was very much in "go" mode, and at his urging, Eric sent the scorecard to the members of the man-

Figure II.38

The InterTech Customer Scorecard

Customer Behavior and Profitability: What if?

Pyramid Position	Last Year's Performance			What if? Changes	What if? Performance			Profit Change $	Profit Change %
	Customers	Revenue	Profit		Customers	Revenue	Profit		
Top	4	566.115	161.586	1	5	707.643	201.982	40.396	25%
Big	18	462.561	95.322	2	20	513.957	105.913	10.591	11%
Medium	68	550.633	76.605	3	71	574.926	79.985	3.380	4%
Small	360	447.674	-96.113	-6	354	440.213	-94.511	1.602	-2%
Inactives/Prospects/Suspects			-145.900				-145.900	0	0%
Totals	450	2,026.983	91.499	0	450	2,236.739	147.469	55.969	61%

Customer Satisfaction Scores

Value Proposition	Satisfaction	Importance	Action
Delivery times	3.3	4.3	Fix Now!
Price/value for money	3.8	4.8	Fix Now!
Meet agreements and deadlines	3.9	4.6	Fix Now!
Speed of technical service	3.9	4.5	Fix Now!
Expertise of technical service	4.0	4.6	Keep it up!
Expertise of Account Manager	4.1	4.4	Keep it up!
Complaint handling	4.1	4.2	Keep it up!
Understand customer's business	4.1	4.9	Keep it up!
Lifetime/durability/robustness	4.1	4.6	Keep it up!
Availability of Account Manger	4.1	4.3	Keep it up!
Ease of installation	4.2	4.4	Keep it up!
Quality of construction	4.2	4.5	Keep it up!
Come up with ideas	3.7	3.8	Fix Later!
Tel./correspondence is friendly	4.1	3.7	Applause!

Customer Focus Scores

Summary	Situation	Priority	"Gap"
Management	0.9	1.6	0.7
Staff	1.0	1.4	0.4
Methods/Media/Message	0.7	1.4	0.6
Contact Logistics	0.8	1.5	0.7
Customer Info	2.1	4.3	2.2
Cust. Info System	1.9	4.4	2.5
Priority Items	**Situation**	**Priority**	**"Gap"**
Mgt. allocates budget	2.6	4.8	2.2
People work in teams.	2.9	4.2	1.3
Best method, low cost.	2.2	4.1	1.9
Contact Plan	2.3	4.5	2.2
Info is Relevant	2.4	4.2	1.8
Info is Complete	2.2	4.4	2.2
Info is up-to-date	1.6	4.3	2.7
System is effective.	1.8	4.5	2.7
System is flexible	1.6	4.3	2.7
System is accessible.	1.8	4.5	2.7

Customer Loyalty Summary

72% will buy in future	51% will give references	8% sole supplier	41% preferred supplier

agement team and project group to serve as the basis for making decisions about next steps.

Make decisions about customer satisfaction/customer focus improvement activities and groups.

A review of your customer satisfaction and customer focus scores and the priorities should make it clear which "challenges" to tackle first.

Then, for key problems (or clusters of problems), you should appoint an Improvement Group.

Improving customer satisfaction or customer focus should be a top-down/bottom-up process in which the Improvement Group will be charged with submitting improvement plans with budgets and, when these are approved, carrying them out. Often the groups are multidepartmental.

InterTech decided to install two Improvement Groups.

- Customer Information Group (CIG)
  The membership of this group was easy to establish—the Customer Marketing Project Group would take on this additional task because they were going to be working hands-on with this subject. They decided, for the short term, to buy an inexpensive contact management system to capture and manage the data from the customer interviews. On the basis of the model project experience, they would be well equipped to specify requirements for a company-wide system. Nils Novotny, Finance and IT Manager, would be ex-officio adviser to the group.

- Speedy Service Group (SSG)
  Representatives from service, logistics, sales, and administration were nominated to resolve the cluster of complaints about "Meet agreements and deadlines," "Delivery times," and "Speed of technical service." The chairman of the group: Production Manager Vincent Brown.

   It was decided that the other issues identified in the customer focus assessment—teamwork contact planning and management time commitment—would probably be (partially) resolved during the model project.

Make decisions about the Customer Teams.

You should select the Customer Team(s) for your company-wide or model project with these criteria in mind:

- The Customer Team members have (or will have) direct or indirect contact with the same set of customers that are represented in a cus-

tomer pyramid: field sales, telephone sales, marketing, service, etc. (It is possible, of course, for some team members—for instance, a service technician—to serve on more than one Customer Team.)
- The Customer Team should have a leader or captain. (In a business-to-business situation, the account or sales manager for a particular territory is often the team leader.).
- The Customer Team should be able to come together for three or four introduction sessions over a period of six to eight weeks during the start-up.

The InterTech Customer Team in the Midwest region consisted of:

- *Joe Epstein, Account Manager*
- *Wyetha Baxter, Telesales*
- *Chris Jerkins, Service Engineer*
- *Mildred Fudd, Order Administration*
- *Alicia Potts, Marketing*

Bill de Vries would serve as their Customer Marketing instructor and mentor. As his first step, he called them together and briefed them officially, but because he had been informing them regularly of the diagnosis and the results, there were no surprises.

Schedule rollout phase activities.

If at all possible, try to schedule your rollout activities to coincide with a business planning period so that you can incorporate the customer planning activities into the official plan. But if this is not possible, don't delay the process.

The key events to schedule in the first six to eight weeks of the rollout period:

- A Customer Marketing Kick-off (company-wide)
- A Customer-Based Business Planning Workshop (one or two days)
- Four Customer Team Workshops (half-day each)

Eric Dines planned the Customer Marketing Kick-off for the next "All Hands on Board" meeting, scheduled in three weeks. The other events were plugged into the corporate agenda.

Are you curious about what happened?
Read on!

Phase IV: Rollout

Figure II.39

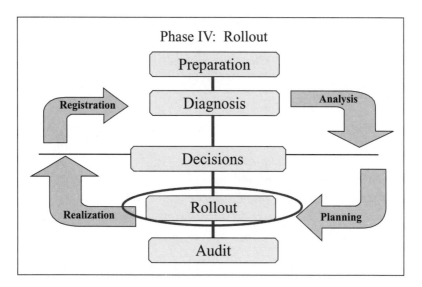

Until now your Customer Marketing activities have been pretty much a desktop exercise involving a limited number of people.

The rollout phase (Figure II.39) means that you will go "live," come out of the closet, and get the involvement of everyone in your company, starting with a Customer Marketing Kick-off.

Other events at the start will be a Customer-Based Business Planning Workshop to develop top-down customer goals and contact plans.

These top-down plans will later be the subject of bottom-up customer planning during Customer Team Workshops.

And then it really starts to happen as the Customer Teams and Improvement Groups go "make it happen"!

Start with a Customer Marketing
Kick-off

The Customer Marketing Kick-off is an event staged for the whole company or business unit to reach these objectives:

- *Dramatize the importance of customers* to the health of the company (and the career opportunities for the employees) by showing the customer pyramids and results of "What if?" simulations.
- *Announce the start of the Customer Marketing rollout*—the objectives and the steps that will be taken.
- *Disseminate the results of the customer satisfaction survey* and announce the formation of any Improvement Groups appointed to fix low scores.
- *Invite the participation of everyone* by asking them to complete the Customer Focus Self-Assessment form (if this has not already been done) and/or submitting "Customer Satisfaction Improvement Ideas" with the promise that all submissions will be read, acknowledged, and considered for prizes awarded to the best ones.
- *Demonstrate management commitment to improving customer relationships* by, for instance, announcing that all senior managers will be required to telephone one customer a day (or week?) to thank the customer for his business and ask him for satisfaction improvement suggestions.

The InterTech Customer Marketing Kick-off took place, of course, at the next AHOB Meeting.

Eric opened the meeting with an explanation of CRM and the Customer Marketing method to implement it, illustrating his talk with InterTech's customer pyramids. He also showed how a modest upgrading of customers could mean substantial profit gains to ensure the continuity of the company (and the jobs of the attendees).

He then turned the show over to Bill de Vries, who presented the results of the Customer Marketing diagnosis and explained what would happen in the rollout phase.

Then Eric came back to announce the installation of Improvement Groups and a customer satisfaction idea program and announced that he and all senior staff would make weekly telephone interviews with customers.

To show his seriousness, Eric made a telephone call from the podium to Bob Struckman, Managing Director of one of InterTech's largest clients, which everyone could hear via the PA system. Eric thanked Bob for his business and asked him what improvement suggestions he had for InterTech.

Bob had been well briefed by Eric and played his role beautifully, making comments—positive and negative—about each InterTech department, naming names of employees when giving positive comments.

The meeting ended with everyone getting a desk clock in the form of a customer pyramid engraved with this message: "Isn't it time to think about our customers?"

Needless to say, the Kick-off was a great success.

Customer-Based Business Planning Workshop

A Customer-Based Business Planning Workshop brings representatives from (top) management, sales management, and marketing management together to set and reach consensus on:

- Top-down company goals: What are your revenues, costs, profit targets?
- Top-down customer goals: How many of which kinds of customers/prospects do you need to identify, create, keep, or upgrade to meet the customer goals?
- Top-down contact plans: What is the optimal mix of methods and media for each customer (type) needed to meet the customer goal at the least possible cost?

If well prepared in advance by the project team, this critical event should take only a day.

Customer-Based Business Planning Workshop Part I:
Set Top-Down Goals for
Every Customer and Prospect

Set Top-Down Company Goals

The management of Customer Marketing companies have the advantage of real-world and customer-based scenarios to work from, such as the "What if?" exercise discussed earlier. Hence the goals for revenues, profits, or market share can be made with the knowledge that there are sufficient numbers of customers and prospects with the potential to reach the targets.

> *Bill de Vries (after a long session with Eric Dines) presented these goals for the InterTech Midwest region based on the "What if?" scenarios developed during the diagnostic phase (see Figure II.40):*

- *A 10% increase in revenues*
- *A 77% increase in profits*
- *A 3% hike in marketing, sales, and overhead costs due to inflation*

Figure II.40

InterTech Results Last Year			InterTech Top-Down Company Goals			Change
Revenues	$2,026,983	100%	Revenues	$2,229,681	100%	10%
Direct Costs	1,183,484	58%	Direct Costs	1,293,215	58%	9%
Margin %	42%		Margin %	42%	0%	0%
Margin	843,499	42%	Margin	936,466	42%	10%
General Overheads	355,000	18%	General Overheads	365,650	16%	3%
Profit before M&S	488,499	24%	Profit before M&S	570,816	26%	14%
Marketing & Sales			Marketing & Sales			
Sales Costs	302,000	15%	Sales Costs	311,060	14%	3%
Marketing Costs	25,000	1%	Marketing Costs	25,750	1%	3%
M&S Overheads	70,000	3%	M&S Overheads	72,100	3%	3%
Total M&S Costs	397,000	20%	Total M&S Costs	408,910	18%	3%
Operational Profit	$91,499	5%	Operational Profit	$161,906	7%	77%
Customers	450		Customers	450		0%
Revenue per Customer	4,504		Revenue per Customer	4,955		10%
Profit per Customer	203		Profit per Customer	360		77%
ROI on M&S	23%		ROI on M&S	40%		72%

Set customer goals for every customer and prospect.

But the revenues (and profits) in the company plan will come from only one source: the company's customers—present, future, and past. So to reach the goals, you have to set goals for each customer to meet the company goal.

The idea that management, marketing, and sales executives can make goals and targets for every customer and prospect in half a day seems preposterous. But it can be done if you have the right information, the right tools, and the experience with customers to make assumptions.

The purpose is not to come up with customer goals that are engraved in granite but to give the sales force and customer teams a helping hand in making their own bottom-up customer goals, which, when negotiated, will form the basis of the company's business plan for the coming period.

There are four methods you can use to make goals and targets for every customer in an afternoon. Let's look to see how they work, assuming you want a 10% revenue increase.

1. *The Last Year Model:*
   You simply add 10% to the revenues last year of each customer. This is, of course, a no-brainer. But if the only data you have on a customer is one year of revenue, there is no other way.

2. *The Historic Model:*
   This method works if you have two or more years of revenue data, but no Total Spend or Customer Share information or factors. You input a weighted average for each year of customer data and then "enforce" the business plan so that the output for each customer will total up to a 10% overall increase in revenue. The problem with this system is that it does not take into account any Total Spend or Customer Share factors.

   Two companies, each with revenues of exactly $10,000, may be targeted for revenues of, let's say, $11,354 for one and $10,874 for the other. But with the first you have a Customer Share of 90% and only 8% with the second customer—more than $90,000 in revenue to go for—but the tool doesn't know that.

3. *The Total Spend–Customer Share Model:*

This method is not complicated, and it's better than the preceding ones because you work with (reasonably) accurate numbers on Total Spend and Customer Share. In this model, to reach the desired revenue level, you can try out Customer Share goals such as

– Increase customer share by 5% of all Top customers.
– Increase customer share by 30% of all Small customers which have a Total Spend equal to that of the Top customers.

4. *The Total Spend–Customer Share Factors Model:*

This is the most complex but most accurate method for setting individual customer goals. With this model you estimate the weights of your Total Spend factors (such as size of company, industry) and Customer Share factors (satisfaction, competition). A highly complex calculation is then made factoring these in with Total Spend and Customer Share data.

The InterTech Project group elected to go for option 3: the Total Spend–Customer Share model. Here are the steps they took.

Calculate Total Spend for next year.

You identified, asked for, calculated, or guessed at the Total Spend of your customers and prospects for last year and some factors that will determine the Total Spend, such as industry or size. Select one or more key factors, make an assumption about the effect on Total Spend next year, and let the spreadsheet do the work.

Industry research reports helped the InterTech workshop conclude that the Total Spend of their customer segments would increase as follows: kitchen appliance manufacturers + 5%; machine tools makers + 4%; and other customers + 3% (see Figure II.41). Finished in no time!

Set Customer Share goals.

Total Spend is one thing—but what share you want to get is a larger Customer Share. If you have a high Customer Share, your goals for in-

Figure II.41

Top-Down Total Spend Estimates for Next Year

Customer Name	Last Year Total Spend	Customer Size	Customer Industry	Top-Down Change	Top-Down Total Spend
Struckman	$592,700	>1,000	M-Tools	4%	$616,408
Boards Unlimited	202,700	500–999	Appliance	5%	212,835
Silicon Sync	529,600	500–999	Appliance	5%	556,080
Green Machine	34,800	250–499	M-Tools	4%	36,192
SpeedServ	151,800	250–499	Other	3%	156,354
Main	13,000	>1,000	M-Tools	4%	13,520
Sentinel Service	18,300	500–999	Appliance	5%	19,215
Colby Corp.	110,000	100–249	Appliance	5%	115,500
Bates Milling	18,900	100–249	Other	3%	19,467
Montpelier SA	7,000	100–249	Other	3%	7,210
de Vries Inc.	4,600	500–999	Other	3%	4,738
Bristol	58,000	500–999	Other	3%	59,740
Wilkes Corp.	45,000	250–499	M-Tools	4%	46,800
Jones & Long	158,000	>1,000	Appliance	5%	165,900
British Techno	43,000	250–499	Appliance	5%	45,150
Cellular Tel	12,000	<100	Other	3%	12,360
Bowdoin Bros.	3,900	500–999	Other	3%	4,017

creasing it should be modest. If you have a low Customer Share, you should be aggressive with your top-down customer goals. Go for it!

After studying the numbers for quite a while, the InterTech project group proposed these guidelines for setting Customer Share goals:

For all customers with a Customer Share of

    more than 75%   *no change*

For all customers with a Customer Share of 51%–75%   *+10%*

For all customers with a Customer Share of 25%–50%   *+30%*

For all customers with a Customer Share of 1%–25%   +100%

Customer Share goal of a reactivated inactive customer   10%

Customer Share goal of a new customer   10%

Figure II.42 shows what happened when they translated these top-down Customer Share goals to the customer selection.

The resulting projection delivered a 35% increase in revenues, far above the corporate goal. But the workshop attendees figured that their top-down goals would no doubt be substantially downsized by the salespeople and customer service reps confronted with them. Plus they did not take into consideration any customer defection or loss due to mergers, bankruptcy, etc.

Customer-Based Business Planning Workshop Part II: Make Top-Down Contact Plans for Every Customer and Prospect

Now you have made all top-down goals for all customers and prospects. That's all well, good, and nice to see.

But how do you get those Small customers to Big status? How much can you afford to spend on a Small customer that will remain Small?

Can you really make a top-down contact plan for every customer and prospect—in a day?

The answer is yes, assuming you have done some homework and come to the party prepared with the right information.

Budget your contact capacity and costs.

The first step is to establish what your marketing and sales contact capacity and costs per contact are. There are two categories of marketing and sales efforts to be considered: *methods and media* and *customer benefits.*

Methods and media are the traditional marketing and sales activities: sales visits, outbound telephone calls, mailings, invitations to seminars and shows.

Customer benefits are those extra items that you offer to your cus-

Figure II.42

InterTech Calculates Top-Down Customer Goals

Customer Name	Last Year Year Revenue	Last Year Customer Share	Last Year Total Spend	Last Year Pyramid Position	Top-Down Total Spend	Top-Down Share Change	Top-Down Customer Share Goal	Top-Down Revenue Target	Top-Down Change %
Struckman	$296,337	50%	$592,700	Top	$616,408	15%	57%	$354,419	20%
Boards Unlimited	$143,945	71%	$202,700	Top	$212,835	15%	82%	$173,814	21%
Silicon Sync	$42,365	8%	$529,600	Big	$556,080	100%	16%	$88,967	110%
Green Machine	$31,010	89%	$34,800	Big	$36,192	0%	89%	$32,250	4%
SpeedServ	$13,659	9%	$151,800	Medium	$156,354	100%	18%	$28,138	106%
Main	$13,026	100%	$13,000	Medium	$13,520	0%	100%	$13,547	4%
Sentinel Service	$12,604	69%	$18,300	Medium	$19,215	15%	79%	$15,219	21%
Colby Corp.	$4,791	4%	$110,000	Small	$115,500	100%	9%	$10,061	110%
Bates Milling	$1,717	9%	$18,900	Small	$19,467	100%	18%	$3,537	106%
Montpelier SA	$680	10%	$7,000	Small	$7,210	100%	19%	$1,401	106%
de Vries Inc.	$97	2%	$4,600	Small	$4,738	100%	4%	$200	106%
Bristol	$0		$58,000	Inactive	$59,740		15%	$8,961	
Wilkes Corp.	$0		$45,000	Inactive	$46,800		15%	$7,020	
Jones & Long	$0		$158,000	Prospect	$165,900		10%	$16,590	
British Techno	$0		$43,000	Prospect	$45,150		10%	$4,515	
Cellular Tel	$0		$12,000	Prospect	$12,360			$0	
Bowdoin Bros.	$0		$3,900	Prospect	$4,017			$0	
Total	**$560,231**	**28%**	**$2,003,300**		**$2,091,486**		**36%**	**$758,638**	**35%**

tomers to improve your relationship, such as the Christmas card (which nobody reads), the Christmas wine (which everybody drinks but doesn't remember who sent it), and the Christmas dinner (which generally has an impact on those who attend).

Since these activities are managed by marketing and sales, it is essential that they do the budgeting effort together.

> *Alicia Potts and Bill de Vries got together to set up the InterTech contact budget for the model project.*
>
> *They proposed these marketing and sales contacts: field sales visits, outbound telesales calls, a mailing program, and invitations to the Widget trade show.*
>
> *The big (and expensive) "customer benefit" for key customers and prospects was an invitation to a professional football game, with all the trimmings. For smaller customers, they decided to try out a Breakfast Surprise that would be delivered to the office of the key contact person. All customers would participate in the Charity Gift program, which entailed a gift by InterTech in the customer's/ prospect's name to a local charity. (The family trust of Eric Dines made the gift, so the model project was charged only for the mailing costs of $2 each.)*
>
> *Figure II.43 shows the results of their effort.*

Figure II.43

InterTech Contact Planning: Capacity and Budgets

Contact Planning	Sales Visits	Telesales Calls	Mailing Program	Show Invites	Charity Gifts	Breakfast Surprise	Football Party	Budget Totals
Contact Capacity	1,000	4,000	5,650	963	500	77	40	12,229
Budget	$202,000	$100,000	$11,300	$7,700	$1,000	$1,000	$4,000	$327,000
Cost Per	$202	$25	$2	$8	$2	$13	$100	$26.74

Make a Standard Contact Plan for every customer/prospect situation.

The next step is to bring to the table the selected wisdom of management, marketing, and sales to make a Standard Contact Plan for every customer/prospect situation.

Figure II.44

InterTech Customer Migration Matrix: What if? Scenario

	This Year	*Top*	*Big*	*Medium*	*Small*	*Inactive*	*Prospects*	*Suspects*
Top	4	3	0	1	0	0	0	0
Big	18	1	9	3	2	2	0	0
Medium	68	1	6	41	18	2	0	0
Small	360	0	2	21	300	37	0	0
Inactive	99	0	3	2	8	87	0	0
Prospects	37	0	1	4	8	0	24	0
Suspects	380	0	0	0	16	0	12	352
Next Year Customers	*450*	*5*	*21*	*72*	*352*			
Next Year Other	*516*					128	36	352

That means you need to make a contact plan for each and every cell in your migration matrix that reflects customer behavior in the future. Since there are seven rows and seven columns (see Figure II.44), you need to make 49 Standard Contact Plans!

It sounds like a lot to do, but it goes quite quickly if you tilt the migration matrix on its side to produce a more logical view as shown in Figure II.45.

It took Alicia and Bill exactly 90 minutes of debate to package their methods, media, and customer benefits into Standard Contact Plans for every cell in the migration matrix, as shown in Figure II.45.

They paid special attention to the allocation of the most expensive—and scarce—resource: field sales visits. No field sales visits were allocated to Small customers that were not targeted to move up the customer pyramid.

The visits were too costly and scarce for this kind of customer, who would be maintained with less expensive telesales and mail contacts.

Calculate your Standard Contact Plan capacity.

Once your Standard Contact Plans have been made for each cell in the migration matrix, you simply multiply the projected number of

Figure II.45

InterTech Standard Contact Plans per Migration Matrix Cell

Plan Position	Customer Goal	Sales Visits	Telesales Calls	Personal Letters	Show Invites	Charity Gifts	Breakfast Surprise	Football Party
TOP								
Top	Keep	12	12	4	1	1		1
Big	Downgrade	8	12	4	1	1		1
Medium	Downgrade	6	9	4	1	1		1
Small	Downgrade	6	6	4	1	1		1
Inactive	Downgrade	4	4	4	1	1		1
BIG								
Top	Upgrade	12	8	4	1	1		1
Big	Keep	8	12	4	1	1		1
Medium	Downgrade	6	9	4	1	1		1
Small	Downgrade	4	6	4	1	1		1
Inactive	Downgrade	4	4	4	1	1		1
MEDIUM								
Top	Upgrade	12	9	6	1	1		1
Big	Upgrade	8	9	6	1	1		1
Medium	Keep	6	12	6	1	1	1	
Small	Downgrade	1	6	6	1	1		
Inactive	Downgrade	2	4	6	1	1		
SMALL								
Top	Upgrade	12	9	8	1	1		1
Big	Upgrade	8	9	8	1	1		1
Medium	Upgrade	6	9	8	1	1	1	
Small	Keep	0	4	8	1	1		
Inactive	Downgrade	0	1	8	1	1		
INACTIVE								
Top	Reactivate	6	6	4	1	1		1
Big	Reactivate	4	6	4	1	1		1
Medium	Reactivate	3	6	4	1	1	1	
Small	Reactivate	1	2	4	1	1		
Inactive	Reactivate	0	0	4	1	1		
PROSPECTS								
Top	Create	12	1	4	1	1		1
Big	Create	12	1	4	1	1		1
Medium	Create	9	1	4	1	1	1	
Small	Create	6	4	4	1	1		
Inactive	Keep	0	4	4	1	1		
SUSPECTS								
Prospects	Identify	0	1	4	1			
Suspects	Keep	0	0	4	1			

customers/prospects in each cell to estimate what marketing and sales resources will be needed to reach the goals—and if you have these resources in your budget.

As you can see in Figure II.46, InterTech will need 752 sales visits and 2,514 outbound telephone calls to complete all the Standard Contact Plans.

Figure II.46

InterTech Standard Contact Plans: Calculating Requirements

Plan Position	Customer Goal	Number of Customer/ Prospects	Sales Visits	Telesales Calls	Personal Letters	Show Invites	Charity Gifts	Breakfast Surprise	Football Party
TOP									
Top	Keep	3	36	36	12	3	3	0	3
Big	Downgrade	0	0	0	0	0	0	0	0
Medium	Downgrade	1	6	9	4	1	1	0	1
Small	Downgrade	0	0	0	0	0	0	0	0
Inactive	Downgrade	0	0	0	0	0	0	0	0
BIG									
Top	Upgrade	1	12	8	4	1	1	0	1
Big	Keep	9	72	108	36	9	9	0	9
Medium	Downgrade	3	18	27	12	3	3	0	3
Small	Downgrade	2	8	12	8	2	2	0	2
Inactive	Downgrade	2	8	8	8	2	2	0	0
MEDIUM									
Top	Upgrade	1	12	9	6	1	1	0	1
Big	Upgrade	6	48	54	36	6	6	0	6
Medium	Keep	41	246	492	246	41	41	41	0
Small	Downgrade	18	18	108	108	18	18	0	0
Inactive	Downgrade	2	4	8	12	2	2	0	0
SMALL									
Top	Upgrade	0	0	0	0	0	0	0	0
Big	Upgrade	2	16	18	16	2	2	0	2
Medium	Upgrade	21	126	189	168	21	21	21	0
Small	Keep	300	0	1,200	2,400	300	300	0	0
Inactive	Downgrade	37	0	37	296	37	37	0	0
INACTIVE									
Top	Reactivate	0	0	0	0	0	0	0	0
Big	Reactivate	3	12	18	12	3	3	0	3
Medium	Reactivate	2	6	12	8	2	2	2	0
Small	Reactivate	8	8	16	32	8	8	0	0
Inactive	Reactivate	87	0	0	348	87	87	0	0
PROSPECTS									
Top	Create	0	0	0	0	0	0	0	0
Big	Create	1	12	1	4	1	1	0	1
Medium	Create	4	36	4	16	4	4	4	0
Small	Create	8	48	32	32	8	8	0	0
Inactive	Keep	24	0	96	96	24	24	0	0
SUSPECTS									
Prospects	Identify	12	0	12	48	12	0	0	0
Suspects	Keep	352	0	0	1,408	352	0	0	0
Totals		950	752	2,514	5,376	950	586	68	32

But there is no problem. Alicia and Bill compared existing resources and capacity for sales visits (1,000) and outbound telephone calls (4,000) and found that the goals could be met in the current budget. (see Figure II.47).

Pleased with their efforts, the InterTech executives retired to the bar to talk about the Customer Team Workshops that were due to start in two weeks.

Figure II.47

InterTech Contact Planning: Capacity and Budgets

Contact Planning	Sales Visits	Telesales Calls	Mailing Program	Show Invites	Charity Gifts	Breakfast Surprise	Football Party	Budget Totals
Contact Capacity	1,000	4,000	5,650	963	500	77	40	12,229
Budget	$202,000	$100,000	$11,300	$7,700	$1,000	$1,000	$4,000	$327,000
Cost Per	$202	$25	$2	$8	$2	$13	$100	$26.74
Needed	**752**	**2,514**	**5,376**	**950**	**586**	**68**	**32**	**10,278**
Cost	$151,904	$62,850	$10,752	$7,600	$1,172	$884	$3,200	$238,362
Capacity Balance	248	1,486	274	13	−86	9	8	1,951
Budget Balance	$50,096	$37,150	$548	$100	−$172	$116	$800	$88,638

Customer Team Workshops

The Customer Team Workshops are a key vehicle for implementing Customer Marketing and CRM in your company.

During four sessions you will walk with the Customer Team through the four phases of Customer Marketing—Registration, Analysis, Planning, and Realization.

You will work with a small and manageable number of real-world customers—the customer selection—and customer information acquired during the Diagnosis.

This process serves as a jump start for the team, which, after the workshop, will apply the same procedures to the remainder of the customers in their pyramid.

Session I: Registration

Thus the first Customer Team Workshop is the first confrontation between your top-down ideas, plans, and goals for Customer Marketing and CRM vs. the bottom-up feelings and attitudes on the part of the people who are supposed to make it happen.

Take it easy at first.

Don't be in a rush. Never underestimate the time needed to transfer an idea or concept from the head of one person to another.

The first session should be low key. Take a lot of time to explain the Customer Marketing method; show the results of the diagnostic phase. Let the group make a customer pyramid with their own customer data as a practice exercise.

Assign homework: a customer interview.

Then start talking about the results of the preliminary customer interviews. Do some role playing with the questionnaire. And then give an assignment before the next session two weeks hence: all hands must conduct at least one customer interview, either face to face or by telephone.

> *Bill de Vries was a bit nervous before the start of the workshop. But as he got into explaining the results of the Customer Marketing diagnosis—and the future plans for the model project—he lost his slight anxiety about what he had gotten into, suggesting such major changes to a company like InterTech.*
>
> *The group responded positively to Bill—until the subject of customer interview came up. Account Manager Joe Epstein seemed especially critical of the idea: "Do we have the time for all of that? Do you really think the customers will give their answers to these questions?" But he calmed down when Bill told him that Eric, Mike Shea, and he himself had conducted trial customer interviews.*
>
> *Wyetha Baxter of telesales had no problem with the idea of doing a customer interview via telephone. But Mildred Fudd of order administration was clearly apprehensive about the idea. However, she agreed to give it a try.*
>
> *The group agreed that all members of the Customer Team would interview a customer before the next session, scheduled a week away.*

Session II: Analysis

Evaluate and review homework: customer interviews.

"How did it go?" That's the key question to start off this and the remaining Customer Team Workshops, all of which require some homework—in this case, the customer interviews.

> *The InterTech customer team was enthusiastic and somewhat amazed that*
>
> - *Customers were willing to do the interview ("Let's talk about me!").*
> - *The interviews lasted about twice as long as planned ("Let's talk about me!!").*

Even the somewhat shy Mildred Fudd scored a telephone interview of 45 minutes—and got an unexpected order of more than $10,000 before she hung up the telephone!

Present—and justify—your top-down customer goals.

This is a moment of truth for most companies. More often than not, salespeople and account managers supply management with a bottom-up estimate of sales revenues from a region or territory without specifying from which customers those revenues will come. Introducing top-down revenue goals specific by customer is likely to generate resistance, protest, and comments such as "Those dumbos and nerds at headquarters don't know anything about customers and selling."

To overcome this resistance, you should always admit up front that the Customer Team members know the customers better than any computer and that the top-down customer goals are *guaranteed to be inaccurate*. But also say that they are *guaranteed to be helpful* in providing the Customer Team with some data and guidelines to analyze the customers and come back with a well-considered and rational bottom-up goal for each customer.

Assign homework: bottom-up customer goals.

Ask the customer team to review the top-down customer goals and come to the next session with their response: bottom-up customer goals.

Bill handed out the top-down customer goals for the customer selection (see Figure II.A) together with the "flat file" database to give the Customer Team up-to-date information on each customer. He left the session earlier to give them some time to discuss the customers without him in the room.

Session III: Planning

Evaluate and review homework: bottom-up customer goals.

The Customer Team should bring to this session their bottom-up customer goals. Any major discrepancies on Total Spend and Customer Spend estimates should, of course, be discussed and justified. But as

Figure II.48A

InterTech Top-Down Customer Goals Proposed at Customer Team Workshop

Customer Name	Last Year Revenue	Last Year Pyramid	Top Down Total Spend	Top Down Share Goal	Top Down Target	Top Down Pyramid	Customer Goal	Top Down Change
Struckman	$296,337	Top	$616,408	57%	$354,419	Top	Keep	20%
Boards Unlimited	$143,945	Top	$212,835	82%	$173,814	Top	Keep	21%
Silicon Sync	$42,365	Big	$556,080	16%	$88,967	Top	Upgrade	110%
Green Machine	$31,010	Big	$36,192	89%	$32,250	Big	Keep	4%
SpeedServ	$13,659	Medium	$156,354	18%	$28,138	Big	Upgrade	106%
Main	$13,026	Medium	$13,520	100%	$13,547	Medium	Keep	4%
Sentinel Service	$12,604	Medium	$19,215	79%	$15,219	Big	Keep	21%
Colby Corp.	$4,791	Small	$115,500	9%	$10,061	Medium	Upgrade	110%
Bates Milling	$1,717	Small	$19,467	18%	$3,537	Small	Keep	106%
Montpelier SA	$680	Small	$7,210	19%	$1,401	Small	Keep	106%
de Vries Inc.	$97	Small	$4,738	4%	$200	Small	Keep	106%
Bristol	$0	Inactive	$59,740	15%	$8,961	Medium	Create	
Wilkes Corp.	$0	Inactive	$46,800	15%	$7,020	Medium	Keep	
Jones & Long	$0	Prospect	$165,900	10%	$16,590	Medium	Create	
British Techno	$0	Prospect	$45,150	10%	$4,515	Small	Create	
Cellular Tel	$0	Prospect	$12,360		$0	Prospect	Keep	
Bowdoin Bros.	$0	Prospect	$4,017		$0	Prospect	Keep	
Total	$560,231		$2,091,486	36%	$758,638			35%

Figure II.48B

Customer Name	Last Year Revenue	Last Year Pyramid	Consensus Total Spend	Consensus Share Goal	Consensus Target	Consensus Pyramid	Customer Goal	Consensus Change
Struckman	$296,337	Top	$500,000	60%	$300,000	Top	Keep	1%
Boards Unlimited	$143,945	Top	$200,000	75%	$150,000	Top	Keep	4%
Silicon Sync	$42,365	Big	$600,000	17%	$100,000	Top	Upgrade	136%
Green Machine	$31,010	Big	$30,000	100%	$30,000	Big	Keep	-3%
SpeedServ	$13,659	Medium	$160,000	22%	$35,000	Big	Upgrade	156%
Main	$13,026	Medium	$15,000	7%	$1,000	Small	Downgrade	-92%
Sentinel Service	$12,604	Medium	$20,000	30%	$6,000	Medium	Keep	-52%
Colby Corp.	$4,791	Small	$115,500	13%	$14,500	Big	Upgrade	203%
Bates Milling	$1,717	Small	$20,000	15%	$3,000	Small	Keep	75%
Montpelier SA	$680	Small	$7,000	29%	$2,000	Small	Keep	194%
de Vries Inc.	$97	Small	$7,000	0%	$0	Inactive	Downgrade	-100%
Bristol	$0	Inactive	$60,000	10%	$6,000	Medium	Create	
Wilkes Corp.	$0	Inactive	$20,000	0%	$0	Inactive	Keep	
Jones & Long	$0	Prospect	$140,000	5%	$7,500	Medium	Create	
British Techno	$0	Prospect	$50,000	8%	$4,000	Small	Create	
Cellular Tel	$0	Prospect	$0		$0	Prospect	Keep	
Bowdoin Bros.	$0	Prospect	$0		$0	Prospect	Keep	
Total	$560,231		$1,944,500	34%	$659,000			18%

long as the team meets or exceeds the company goals with their targets, it is best to reach consensus as quickly as possible.

> *The team had obviously spent a lot of time working on both the Total Spend and Customer Share. At the end of the exercise, they came back with customer goals that would produce 18% more revenue—half of the top-down goals but almost twice as much as the company goals of a 10% revenue increase. Bill de Vries agreed on the spot to go with their proposal (see Figure II.48B).*

Present—and justify—your top-down contact plans.

The resistance to top-down contact plans may be even more intense than to customer goals—especially from field salespeople, who have traditionally made the decision about which customer they will visit, how often, and when. You should admit that only the Customer Team members know what the optimal frequency of sales visits per customer should be. But you should also point out that if there is no big potential in a customer, there is no sense in spending a lot of sales time with that customer. To illustrate the point, refer to the famous bank robber Willie Sutton, who was once asked why he robbed banks. His answer: "That's where the money is!"

> *Bill presented the top-down contact plans that had been generated for the customer selection (see Figure II.49).*
> *"What! No way!" was the initial response from Joe Epstein. Again Bill reminded him that the top-down contact plans were simply an aid to help the Customer Team in making their own plans.*

Assign homework: Bottom-up contact plans.

By this time the Customer Team should anticipate the homework: review top-down contact plans and come to the next session with their bottom-up contact plans.

Session IV: Realization

Evaluate and Review homework: bottom-up contact plans.

Review the bottom-up contact plans primarily to see if there are any

Figure II.49

InterTech Top-Down Contact Plans

Customer Name	Last Year Pyramid	Target Pyramid	Sales Visits	Telesales Calls	Personal Letters	Show Invites	Charity Gifts	Breakfast Surprise	Football Party
Struckman	Top	Top	12	12	4	1	1	0	1
Boards Unlimited	Top	Top	12	12	4	1	1	0	1
Silicon Sync	Big	Top	12	8	4	1	1	0	1
Green Machine	Big	Big	8	12	4	1	1	0	1
SpeedServ	Medium	Big	8	9	6	1	1	0	1
Main	Medium	Small	1	6	6	1	1	0	0
Sentinel Service	Medium	Medium	6	12	6	1	1	1	0
Colby Corp.	Small	Big	8	9	8	1	1	0	1
Bates Milling	Small	Small	0	4	8	1	1	0	0
Montpelier SA	Small	Small	0	4	8	1	1	0	0
de Vries Inc.	Small	Inactive	0	1	8	1	1	0	0
Bristol	Inactive	Medium	3	6	4	1	1	1	0
Wilkes Corp.	Inactive	Inactive	0	0	4	1	1	0	0
Jones & Long	Prospect	Medium	9	1	4	1	1	1	0
British Techno	Prospect	Small	6	4	4	1	1	0	0
Cellular Tel	Prospect	Prospect	0	1	4	1	0	0	0
Bowdoin Bros.	Prospect	Prospect	0	0	4	1	0	0	0

discrepancies between plans and capacity. Also keep an eye on the amount of attention given to small customers with low potential.

Bill had no problems with the bottom-up contact plans (see Figure II.50.) And he was pleased to note that the team was getting more positive to this structured way of working.

Assign customer managers.

The Customer Team must assign one of its members to be a "customer manager" who has primary responsibility to ensure that the customer goal is met. The assignments are made to match the customer situation with the skills, availability, and time requirements of the team member. The customer manager can also change if the customer situation changes.

The account manager, Joe Epstein, initially had difficulty giving responsibility for "his customer" to somebody else—especially Mildred Fudd of order administration. But as Bill stressed the advantages for Joe (more time to score bigger orders) and Joe saw how Mildred started to glow with her new responsibility and "empowerment," he capitulated. "OK, let's do it. We can always change customer managers if we need to." (See Figure II.51.)

Put the appointments in the agenda.

This is the time that a contact manager or some form of marketing and sales system is essential. The customer managers are responsible for making visits and telephone calls over a period of time. It is possible to do this with paper-based customer cards (they never crash!), but it is a real problem to make changes and share information. And it is impossible for anyone—especially sales managers—to check how many of which kinds of customer contacts were actually made.

Mildred Fudd was "volunteered" to be in charge of the contact manager Eric Dines had purchased for the customer team. Since it was a single-user system, Mildred would do the contact plan-

Figure II.50

InterTech Customer Contact Plans As Agreed by Customer Teams

Customer Name	Last Year Pyramid	Target Pyramid	Sales Visits	Telesales Calls	Personal Letters	Show Invites	Charity Gifts	Breakfast Surprise	Football Party
Struckman	Top	Top	10	10	4	1	1	0	1
Boards Unlimited	Top	Top	12	12	4	1	1	1	1
Silicon Sync	Big	Top	15	8	4	1	1	0	1
Green Machine	Big	Big	8	6	4	1	1	0	1
SpeedServ	Medium	Big	8	12	6	1	1	0	1
Main	Medium	Small	1	6	6	1	1	0	0
Sentinel Service	Medium	Medium	6	12	6	1	1	0	1
Colby Corp.	Small	Big	8	9	8	1	1	0	1
Bates Milling	Small	Small	0	4	8	1	1	0	0
Montpelier SA	Small	Small	0	4	8	1	1	0	0
de Vries Inc.	Small	Inactive	0	0	0	0	0	0	0
Bristol	Inactive	Medium	3	6	4	1	1	1	0
Wilkes Corp.	Inactive	Inactive	0	0	4	1	1	0	0
Jones & Long	Prospect	Medium	4	1	4	1	1	1	0
British Techno	Prospect	Small	6	4	4	1	1	0	0
Cellular Tel	Prospect	Prospect	0	1	4	1	0	0	0
Bowdoin Bros.	Prospect	Prospect	0	0	4	1	0	0	0

Figure II.51

InterTech Customer Manager Assignments

Customer Name	Last Year Pyramid	Target Pyramid	Customer Manager Name, Function
Struckman	Top	Top	Joe, Sales
Boards Unlimited	Top	Top	Joe, Sales
Silicon Sync	Big	Top	Joe, Sales
Green Machine	Big	Big	Wyetha, Telesales
SpeedServ	Medium	Big	Joe, Sales
Main	Medium	Small	Wyetha, Telesales
Sentinel Service	Medium	Medium	Chris, Service
Colby Corp.	Small	Big	Joe, Sales
Bates Milling	Small	Small	Mildred, Admin.
Montpelier SA	Small	Small	Chris, Service
de Vries Inc.	Small	Inactive	Mildred, Admin.
Bristol	Inactive	Medium	Wyetha, Telesales
Wilkes Corp.	Inactive	Inactive	Alicia, Marketing
Jones & Long	Prospect	Medium	Joe, Sales
British Techno	Prospect	Small	Wyetha, Telesales
Cellular Tel	Prospect	Prospect	Alicia, Marketing
Bowdoin Bros.	Prospect	Prospect	Alicia, Marketing

ning and registration for the team, working from their e-mail messages. It was not very handy, but the CIG (Customer Information Group) promised to come up with a solution before too long.

Don't forget coaching!

You don't implement a whole new way of working in four day-long or half-day sessions. You have to keep working with the Customer Team, giving them encouragement, resolving inevitable territorial battles, making sure they do the right things the right way. But then, that's the job of a manager!

Bill de Vries reported to Eric Dines the successful completion of the Customer Team Workshop and promised to monitor progress closely. Eric agreed to monthly progress reports and remarked that he would look after the progress of the improvement groups.

Monitor Rollout Results

As you might expect with a "measure and manager" method like Customer Marketing, close monitoring of results vs. plan is expected. But you may find it easier than before because the metrics are known and the methods to measure them are in place.

Monitor customer value results.

Meeting customer value targets is the result of realizing all other business plans—plus a healthy portion of good luck!

There are no magic tricks here. It's just a question of monthly/quarterly financial reporting, keeping in consideration the customer-related numbers of revenue and profit per customer, plus the ROI on marketing and sales.

> *Bill presented his half-year financial report (see Figure II.52). Although slightly down vs. plan, he was clearly going to bring in record profits. At the halfway point he had reached almost $75,000 against last year's total profit of $91,000!*

Monitor customer behavior results.

Since operational profits result from positive customer behavior, you will generally find that progress (or lack thereof) runs parallel to customer value monitoring.

But the big difference is the reporting at the customer level, whereby the Customer Teams can see whether or not they are on target for each individual customer.

Figure II.52

InterTech Rollout Monitor: Customer Value

InterTech Plan: Six Months		% Revenues
Revenues	**$1,114,841**	**100%**
Direct Costs	**646,608**	**58%**
Margin %	42%	0%
Margin	**468,233**	**42%**
General Overheads	**182,825**	**16%**
Profit before M&S	**285,408**	**26%**
Marketing & Sales		
Sales Costs	155,530	14%
Marketing Costs	12,875	1%
M&S Overheads	36,050	3%
Total M&S Costs	**204,455**	**18%**
Operational Profit	**$80,953**	**7%**

InterTech Reality: Six Months		Variance	Variance %
Revenues	**$1,123,458**	**$8,617**	**1%**
Direct Costs	**660,939**	**14,331**	**2%**
Margin %	41%	-1%	-2%
Margin	**462,519**	**-5,714**	**-1%**
General Overheads	**183,496**	**671**	**0%**
Profit before M&S	**279,023**	**-6,385**	**-2%**
Marketing & Sales			
Sales Costs	154,729	-801	-1%
Marketing Costs	11,849	-1,026	-8%
M&S Overheads	37,653	1,603	4%
Total M&S Costs	**204,231**	**-224**	**0%**
Operational Profit	**$74,792**	**-$6,161**	**-8%**

Bill was really pleased the way his team was managing the relationships with their customers. And Mildred Fudd was doing well! (See Figure II.53.)

Monitor customer contact results.

Customer behavior is highly dependent on the amount of time, energy, and attention paid to each customer. And that means that the Customer Teams must accomplish the customer contacts and customer benefits per customer. A quarterly or six-month check of what has been accomplished vs. what was planned is essential.

Mildred really struggled with the contact manager system. It was not very user-friendly to begin with, and the communications with her team members cost a lot of time and energy. But she soldiered on and presented two reports to Bill (see Figure II.54.)

Monitor customer satisfaction results.

You will, of course, immediately fix any major dissatisfaction problems with individual customers when they show up on the survey. But it's not a bad idea to call that customer again after six months to see if the problem has stayed fixed—and show that you really care all the time, not just when you get a complaint.

At the same time, you should monitor the progress of the Improvement Group charged with resolving issues that were less than satisfactory across the board.

Silicon Sync had service problems, and customer Main was unhappy with the relationship. Eric called them and was happy to hear that they were happy.

He also asked for a briefing from the Speedy Service Group (SSG) charged with fixing complaints about "Meet agreements and deadlines," "Delivery times," and "Speed of technical service." As might be expected from a production guy who knows statistical process control techniques, Vincent Brown had improved numbers on turnaround times and response times to prove his point. Eric praised his work and asked to remeasure the satisfaction of those who were dissatisfied.

Figure II.53

InterTech Customer Behavior Monitor: Six Months

Customer Name	Customer Goal	Agreed Target		Target to Date		Realised to Date		Prognosis			Who's in Charge?
		Target Pyramid	Target Revenue	Percent Revenue	Target Revenue	Percent Revenue	Actual Revenue	Prognosis Revenue	Revenue Variance	Projection Pyramid	Customer Manager Name, Function
Struckman	Keep	Top	$300,000	47%	$141,000	57%	$171,000	$330,000	$30,000	Top	Joe, Sales
Boards Unlimited	Keep	Top	150,000	47%	70,500	42%	62,500	142,000	–8,000	Top	Joe, Sales
Silicon Sync	Upgrade	Top	100,000	47%	47,000	46%	45,553	98,553	–1,447	Top	Joe, Sales
Green Machine	Keep	Big	30,000	47%	14,100	51%	15,300	31,200	1,200	Big	Wyetha, Telesales
SpeedServ	Upgrade	Big	35,000	47%	16,450	24%	8,400	26,950	–8,050	Big	Joe, Sales
Main	Downgrade	Small	1,000	47%	470	50%	500	1,030	30	Small	Wyetha, Telesales
Sentinel Service	Keep	Medium	6,000	47%	2,820	110%	6,600	9,780	3,780	Medium	Chris, Service
Colby Corp.	Upgrade	Big	14,000	47%	6,580	43%	6,020	13,440	–560	Medium	Joe, Sales
Bates Milling	Keep	Small	3,500	47%	1,645	56%	1,960	3,815	315	Small	Mildred, Admin.
Montpelier SA	Keep	Small	2,000	47%	940	60%	1,200	2,260	260	Small	Chris, Service
de Vries Inc.	Downgrade	Inactive									Mildred, Admin.
Bristol	Create	Medium	6,000	47%	2,820	35%	2,100	5,280	–720	Small	Wyetha, Telesales
Wilkes Corp.	Keep	Inactive								Inactive	Alicia, Marketing
Jones & Long	Create	Medium	7,500	47%	3,525	48%	3,600	7,575	75	Medium	Joe, Sales
British Techno	Create	Small	4,000	47%	1,880	59%	2,360	4,480	480	Small	Wyetha, Telesales
Cellular Tel	Keep	Prospect								Prospect	Alicia, Marketing
Bowdoin Bros.	Keep	Prospect								Prospect	Alicia, Marketing
Total			$659,000	47%	$309,730	50%	$327,093	$676,363	$17,363	3%	

Figure II.54

InterTech Customer Contact Monitor: Six-Month Variances
(0 = on target; – = below target; + = above target)

Customer Name	Last Year Pyramid	Target Pyramid	Sales Visits	Telesales Calls	Personal Letters	Show Invites	Charity Gifts	Breakfast Surprise	Football Party
Struckman	Top	Top	–3	1	0	0			
Boards Unlimited	Top	Top	1	–1	0	0		0	
Silicon Sync	Big	Top	–6	0	0	0			
Green Machine	Big	Big	4	0	0	0			
SpeedServ	Medium	Big	0	–2	0	0			
Main	Medium	Small	0	0	0	0			
Sentinel Service	Medium	Medium	–4	–4	0	0			
Colby Corp.	Small	Big	0	6	0	0			
Bates Milling	Small	Small	0	0	0	0			
Montpelier SA	Small	Small	0	2	0	0			
de Vries Inc.	Small	Inactive	0	0	0	0			
Bristol	Inactive	Medium	–1	0	–1	0		0	
Wilkes Corp.	Inactive	Inactive	0	0	0	0			
Jones & Long	Prospect	Medium	0	0	–1	0		0	
British Techno	Prospect	Small	–1	–1	0	0			
Cellular Tel	Prospect	Prospect	0	0	0	0			
Bowdoin Bros.	Prospect	Prospect	0	0	0	0			

Monitor customer focus results.

Making measurable improvements on customer focus issues takes some time. But that does not excuse you from keeping close tabs on the improvement groups and their activities, asking for monthly reports and, when possible, remeasurements.

Eric Dines was very satisfied with the rollout results so far—with one exception.

There was no progress on solving the customer information system problem. Poor Mildred Fudd was going nuts with a single-user contact manager for a group of four people!

The Customer Information Group (CIG) had been a mistake. The project team was too wrapped up with other things to come up with a proposal for improvement. And Nils Novotny, who was great with bookkeeping systems, just didn't seem to understand what customer information was all about.

Maybe if . . .

Suddenly Bill de Vries and Jo Epstein burst into Eric's office.

"Boss, we are in real trouble! Bob Struckman called me today to say that he heard about some Widgets and Whamos being offered on the Internet—at a price we can hardly afford to meet.

"If we don't do something right away, we're going to lose that customer!"

Eric promised to do something—fast. But he was only certain of one thing: he needed to know a lot more about the Internet and what it could mean for InterTech.

Part Three

Customer Marketing and the Internet

Editor's Note:

In June 1995, Jay Curry, originator of the Customer Marketing method, was helping larger European companies to implement Customer Relationship Management, even though CRM had not yet become a buzzword.

Also in June 1995, Adam Curry was starting to help larger U.S. corporations to "get on the net" with Web site consulting, design, development, and management services. Adam invited Jay to conduct a mini seminar on Customer Marketing for his Management team.

The Currys learned something from each other on that day.

- Jay learned from Adam *the incredible potential of the Internet for prospecting.* Adam's company had created 72,000 e-mail prospects in response to a special offer for a telecommunications company at a cost of only $22,500, or 30 cents per lead, including creative, outgoing e-mail, incoming e-mail and fulfillment. Jay made a quick calculation—about a 1,000% lower cost for a similar campaign using "snail mail"!
- Adam learned from Jay *the incredible potential of the Internet for keeping and upgrading current customers.* Jay asked Adam and his staff what percentage of visitors at a Web site for a brand of sports shoes were current buyers vs. nonbuyers of the shoes. The Web site whiz kids answered: "We don't know—and the clients have never asked us. But we will find out!" As you might expect, they discovered that most of the

visitors at the Web site were current customers—and the communication cost with these customers was only pennies per contact, a cost-per-contact rate that was heretofore unthinkable for producers of consumer goods.

Since that day five years ago, Jay and Adam Curry have engaged in a running dialogue via e-mail, telephone, and face-to-face visits over the relationship of Customer Marketing and the Internet.

To help Eric Dines solve his problems, we arranged "virtual conversations" through which he could discuss with Jay and Adam his concerns about the Internet and Customer Marketing.

The edited transcripts form Part Three of this book.

Eric: We have been working with Customer Marketing. And now we are confronted with the Internet. How do the two fit together? Or do they?

Jay:

I don't think I will ever again write a book or article about Customer Marketing that will have a separate section on the Internet. Customer Marketing and the Internet are becoming so closely entwined that it simply won't make sense.

But a separate section on the Internet is needed in this unique time of change and transition.

Eric, you are one of thousands of CEOs who are wrestling with two questions:

• How can we improve the relationships with our customers?
• What should we do with the Internet?

I suggest that Customer Marketing, Customer Relationship Management, and the Internet are inseparable issues for two main reasons:

1. *The Internet helps solve some major and universal problems related to Customer Relationship Management.* This inexpensive technology is perfectly suited to capturing, analyzing, and using customer information.

2. *The Internet makes Customer Relationship Management a necessity.* If you don't manage the relationship with your customers in the face of Internet-based competition, you will simply go out of business.

Concerning the first point: I have been involved with hundreds of Customer Focus Self-Assessment exercises. Without exception, managers and staff have said this about their customer information and systems:

- We *do not have the right information* to determine customer potential and to communicate with the right customer, about the right product, at the right time.
- Our customer information is *incomplete.*
- Our customer information is *not up-to-date.*
- Our customer information system *does not make it easy* to analyze customers and communicate with them via mail, telephone, and face to face.
- Our customer information system is *inflexible.*
- Our customer information system *does not make available information* about customers to anyone who needs it.

Eric, your customer focus scores were pretty bad in the area of customer information and systems. But as Adam will tell you, the Internet fixes all these problems. Right?

Adam:
Never trust anybody in the IT world who says, "We can fix that problem for you in no time"!

In my experience, if technology is not fixing a current problem, it is more than likely creating a new one. Now that marketing and technology are forever joined through communication and distribution methods such as the Internet, they are creating positive change.

The Internet can help you solve your customer information and system "challenges." And as we go along, I hope to show you how the Internet can deliver to InterTech:

- Information that is useful for determining customer potential and communicating with the right customer, about the right product, at the right time.

- Customer information that fills up a lot of empty spaces you now have.
- Customer information that is updated constantly, in real time.
- A system that makes it easier to analyze customers and communicate with them via several communications methods, including mail, telephone, and face-to-face.
- A system that, unlike the legacy mainframes—and even the most intricate stand-alone PC boxes—can be rapidly changed, at less cost, to meet the changes in the marketplace.
- A system that can distribute customer information to anyone and everyone in your company who needs it, using universal and relatively easy-to-use Web browser technology.

Jay:

Let's turn to the second issue: the Internet creates a situation in which many companies that don't implement CRM will go out of business.

You will recall that the main business of a company is to create and keep customers and to maximize customer profitability.

Customer acquisition—and especially customer retention—was easier when your customers more or less had to do business with you because you were close by. Or because they didn't have the capability to compare prices with suppliers all over the world.

The Internet changes all of that. Your customers, Eric, can get quotes from producers all over the world, and order directly, as you have discovered. The middlemen, the wholesalers and distributors, like you, are really caught in the middle. What is your added value in the supply chain?

Even the producers are having a problem. As I understand it, GE gangs up with other buyers to pool purchases and make gigantic orders—with gigantic discounts—from industrial suppliers around the globe.

It looks like many companies are in the same situation the railroad companies were at the turn of the century, as Theodore Levitt pointed out.

The railroad companies thought they were in the business of running trains, not in the transportation business. Automobile, truck, bus, and airplane companies took their customers away simply because the railroads did not consider the threat of new transportation Technologies.

But don't panic yet, Eric. You have a stable customer base. And you will be able to keep these customers if you manage the relationship properly.

Because, as you have seen for yourself, if your customers are satisfied with you, they will buy from you, buy a lot from you, and buy from you for a long period of time—without a lot of marketing and sales energy.

The result will be high customer—and company—profitability.

The key is asking your customers what they want, how you can move them up your customer pyramid—and then making it happen. Just like Jan de Boer.

In summary, the Internet is a paradox:

- The Internet is a threat to your business because your customers can get instant information about (often cheaper) offerings from your competitors all over the world.
- The Internet is an opportunity for your business because it will help you understand and communicate with customers better than ever.

Adam:

But don't be surprised if the Internet causes you to change your "business model," an Internet buzzword that roughly translates as the mix of products and services for which customers transfer money from their bank account to yours on a (someday) profitable basis.

Of course, you must stick to the core mission of acquiring customers, keeping those customers, and keeping them profitably.

Interestingly enough, you, too, can create great value for your customers, Eric, by aggregating the power of all your customers, just as GE does. But your cost of acquiring customers can be a fraction of that of a behemoth such as GE. Using the Internet appropriately can result in a huge scale of knowledgeable customers, all looking for the best price, as well as better service. If you can develop an online customer base by providing added value service right through your Web site, you can quickly reap the rewards of an "e-business model."

IBM was talked about earlier as a punch-card company that changed their business model into data processing business because Tom Watson, Jr., listened to his customers.

Today IBM is earning major profits, not by selling boxes, but by providing consulting and services. A major part of this new business model is providing e-commerce services to companies that want to identify, make, keep, and upgrade customers—with the Internet!

Eric: Does the Internet affect the customer pyramids?

Jay:
A customer is a customer, and no matter where they come from, customers fit in the normal customer pyramid. But the Internet has added some new dimensions to the customer pyramid concept.

Adam started the ball rolling with his "permission pyramid," derived from his years as a user of the Internet to sell products and services, and as an adviser and service supplier to major companies that wanted to do likewise. Plus some inspiration from Seth Godin's "Permission Marketing" concept (The Free Press, 1999).

Adam:
In the early 1980s, as the Internet started to grow and expand, users spoke of "Nettiquette," or "how to behave online." The concept of "spamming" news groups or large e-mail lists was then like standing in the middle of a cocktail party and yelling:

"HEY, LISTEN TO ME!! I CAN SHOW YOU HOW TO MAKE 10 GRAND A MONTH FROM YOUR HOME!!!"

In those "good old days" everyone tried to self-regulate marketing, advertising, and the general commercialization of "The Net."
Guess what . . . we all failed.

Not that we stood any chance of holding back the spam, the signal-to-noise ratio in news groups, or the mounds of drivel splashed in our faces as banners, buttons, and other marketing messages on the Web.

But here we are. In the next three to five years an estimated three million businesses and organizations in the U.S. alone will establish a presence on the World Wide Web. Even more companies will integrate interactive technologies into the way they do business. Why? Because over 100 million consumers are using the Internet and other interactive technologies, and more are coming online.

So the prospects are out there. But what is the most effective way to speak to them through these new two-way channels?

We have seen some of the world's most famous brick-and-mortar companies get trounced by online competition such as Amazon, Yahoo, and Netscape.

Why do these companies have a competitive edge?

Because they understand that it is important not only how to speak to customers but also how to listen.

The networked economy allows for a dialogue that is changing customer relationships significantly. Customers and prospects now have a way to "speak up and talk back." So we must be careful about the way we conduct a dialogue with them.

It is easy to send off an e-mail offering our products and services to 50,000 names we bought for a song. But there is no guarantee our targeted prospects will open the e-mail we send to them. Or worse, they will be offended because we sent this information unsolicited, effectively cluttering up their mailbox just as badly as spam marketers selling access to porn sites.

E-mail makes it easy to alienate many thousands of people in a short time and at a low cost. (It's a beautiful world isn't it?)

We can also lose a lot of money and goodwill with banners and buttons on Web pages. Like a television or print advertisement, the banners and buttons are meant to entice the user to "click-through" to the product/service shown. For many Internet entrepreneurs they are a simple way to participate in the new connected economy.

Qualitative studies with consumers in focus groups have shown that the human brain now views banners and buttons as layout elements on a Web page—not as advertising. Our eyes go directly to the information we are looking for. We simply ignore or block out banners and buttons.

What is the result? In the Internet world we now have to ask and receive *permission* from individual customers or prospects to speak and build our relationship with them.

- If we send people unsolicited e-mail, we can expect many of them to make it their business to jam up our server for days with anti-spam activities.
- If we use sneaky tricks to push our advertising through news groups, moderators and other watchdogs will make very nasty comments questioning the species of our parents.
- There is no way on earth we can force anyone to visit our Web site. And when somebody does visit it, we must be very, very careful

Figure III.1

The Permission Pyramid

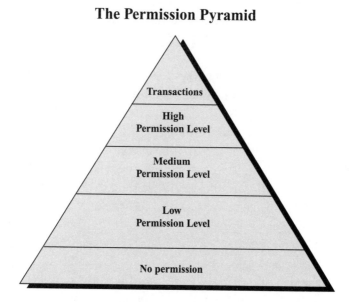

Transactions

High
Permission Level

Medium
Permission Level

Low
Permission Level

No permission

about how we ask them to tell us what they really want to know—
and what they are looking to buy.
- But if we are honest—and clever—we can gradually deepen the
virtual relationship with Web site visitors and get their permission
to build the relationship further. In other words, to get them up . . .
the permission pyramid!

The permission pyramid is a 180-degree turnaround of the customer pyramid (see Figure III.1):

- The customer pyramid represents *the company's view of the individuals* to whom it provides or offers products and services.
- The permission pyramid represents the *individual's view of the
companies* that provide or offer him or her products and services.

Everybody has a permission pyramid for different kinds of companies and categories. Think about your own permission pyramid for,
say companies that offer office supplies.

Starting at the bottom and moving up the permission pyramid:

Figure III.2

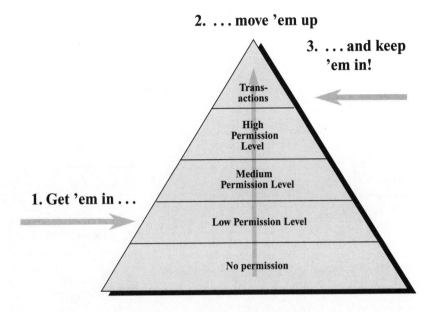

- *No Permission Level:* You want nothing to do with these companies.
- *Low Permission Level:* You don't really know these suppliers, but you might want to look at their offerings and prices.
- *Medium Permission Level:* These companies are known to you. You have neutral feelings about them, and you are not sure you want to spend any time in a dialogue with them. But if they asked politely, you would probably let them send you a catalog or flyer.
- *High Permission Level:* You haven't yet done any business with these suppliers. But you are confident they will send you something relevant and interesting to see, read, or hear. You are not reluctant to give them a lot of data about yourself to get some interesting offers or a special catalog.
- *Transaction Level:* You do transactions with these suppliers. You are a customer. You are satisfied with their products and services. You trust them. And they don't hassle you or clutter up your mailbox with junk mail.

The trick, obviously, is to obtain a slot as high as is relevant on each individual's permission pyramid, as shown in Figure III.2.

Figure III.3

The Swerver Pyramid

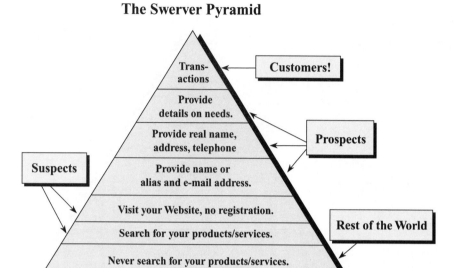

The problem with the permission pyramid is that it is very subjective and based on the feelings and semantics of individuals, not their actual behavior.

Jay:
But we resolved that problem in a conversation we had on . . . let me see . . . December 28, 1998.

Adam:
You're right! On that afternoon we translated "permission levels" to measurable Internet behavior and came up with the "Swerver pyramid" (see Figure III.3).

The "Swerver," of course, is an Internet user whose behavior in relationship to your Web site can be measured—and to some degree managed:

- If the Swerver has absolutely no interest in your products, he or she is "The Rest of the World."
- The Swerver who searches for your category and/or visits your Web site without (knowingly) leaving behind any information can be considered a "Suspect."

Figure III.4

Customer Pyramid: E-Commerce

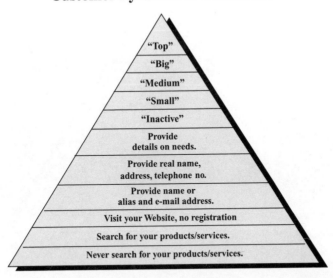

- Swervers who identify themselves and provide information are "Prospects."
- A Swerver who makes some kind of transaction—the ultimate in permission land—is a "Customer."

Jay:
While the Swerver pyramid was on the right track, it seemed to me to be too much focused on noncustomers.

Adam:
So that's when we carried it one step further to arrive at . . . the e-commerce pyramid (see Figure III.4).
   And the obvious e-commerce battle cry (see Figure III.5)!

Eric: I am really worried that we will lose some business and customers because of the Internet. What should we do immediately to defend ourselves and to lay the groundwork for our own Internet operation?

Jay:
Your number-one priority is to protect your customer base. Make an appointment immediately with Bob Struckman and your top 20% cus-

Figure III.5

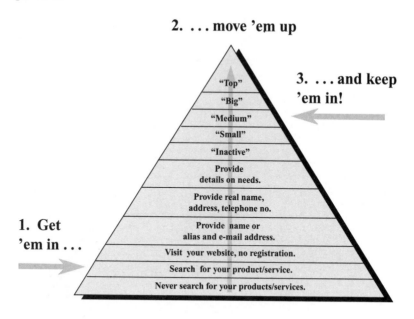

tomers for a follow-up to your customer interview. Or invite a number of good customers to lunch to participate in a group discussion about the Internet. Find out what your customers' views on the Internet are in general and what they want from you specifically. For instance:

- Details on your products and services
- Ordering your products
- Getting technical support
- Tracing the status of orders and shipments
- Other information or service needs

This activity will serve two purposes. First, you will find out what they want, and this will help you develop your Internet strategy and tactics. Second, you will demonstrate your commitment to use Internet technology to meet their needs and get them involved in the process. If they are in collaboration mode, they will be less likely to defect.

Unlike in an e-commerce start-up, your priorities should be represented as shown in Figure III.6.

What are your views on this, Adam?

Figure III.6

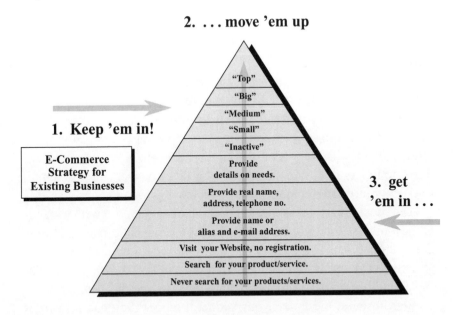

2. . . . move 'em up

1. Keep 'em in!

E-Commerce
Strategy for
Existing Businesses

**3. get
'em in . . .**

"Top"
"Big"
"Medium"
"Small"
"Inactive"
Provide
details on needs.
Provide real name,
address, telephone no.
Provide name or
alias and e-mail address.
Visit your Website, no registration.
Search for your product/service.
Never search for your products/services.

Adam:

Some companies start up with an Intranet—an internal Internet system—to communicate and spread information throughout the company. This tactic serves two purposes:

- It gives your IT people a chance to learn how to manage Internet technologies.
- It gives your managers and staff a way to learn how to use Internet technologies, especially if you insist that expense account reporting and other money-related activities have to go through the Intranet channel.

But the simplest way to start achieving customer-related and other external benefits from the Internet is through the use of e-mail. E-mail allows direct distribution of raw knowledge and information—and highly personal promotional offers to a particular segment of your customer pyramid through a mass e-mail.

There are many tools available that will allow you to send customized e-mail to a list that can virtually contain as many names and e-mail addresses as you wish. Your computer won't really care; it'll just take longer. And the cost, compared to snail mail, is almost nothing.

This type of tool will allow you to send communications that will look very personal to your customers and prospects, using such variables as *first name, customer #,* etc. to give the impression the e-mail was sent to that individual only. This, of course, also depends on your writing style!

Your sales force can also achieve great benefit from e-mail. They can "check in" from virtually anywhere . . . via a laptop, but also through a range of wireless devices, terminals placed in airports, or even on the premises of another customer! Using e-mail can greatly reduce the sales cycle by eliminating the "dog ate my homework" excuse; no longer does one have to rely on faxes, voice, and postal mail to quickly turn around inquiries and orders.

The most important factor to take into consideration with a stand-alone e-mail setup is your company's naming convention for electronic communications. This means that there must be a logical layout and structure in your electronic addressing scheme. In this case we are talking about the two parts of an e-mail address: before the @ and after.

Starting with the latter, your "domain name," you can register it for a nominal fee through Network Solutions in Virginia at *www. networksolutions.com.* You will want to obtain the *.com* address for your company name, brand, or trademark. Because of the global nature of the Net, you may find that another entity, completely unrelated to your business, may already have registered *yourcompanyname.com.* In this case you can check on the availability of another spelling or *.net* and *.org* suffixes.

For individual addresses, the part preceding the @, it is advisable to make multiple entries, or "aliases."

An alias is an electronic forwarding system that enables e-mail sent to one name to go to multiple people. For instance, *sales@intertech.com* might go to the sales desk with a copy to the VP of sales. Likewise, you can create multiple entities that point to one person, such as *eric.dines@intertech.com* and *ceo@intertech.com* that can all deliver e-mail to your personal e-mail in-box!

Eric: I'm pretty handy with Microsoft Office-type programs, but I really don't have a grasp of Internet technology. As CEO, what do I really need to know *and what for me would be* nice to know.

Jay:
Adam, this one is all yours!

Adam:

In my experience in helping CEOs like you deal with the Internet, I have discovered that there are three key technology issues or concepts that are really useful for you to understand:

1. The Internet standards have created a universal network into which every company and human being in the world can be connected.
2. The basic architecture of your Internet Web site.
3. Profiling technology and protocols that generate highly valuable information on your customers and prospects.

Once you understand these concepts, you will know how Internet technology can deliver to InterTech:

- Information that is useful for determining customer potential and communicating with the right customer, about the right product, at the right time.
- Customer information that fills up a lot of empty spaces you now have.
- Customer information that is updated constantly.
- A system that makes it easier to analyze customers and communicate with them via mail, telephone, and face-to-face.
- A system that, unlike the legacy mainframes—and even the most modern PC boxes—can be rapidly changed, at less cost, to meet the changes in the marketplace.
- A system that can distribute customer information to anyone and everyone in your company who needs it, using universal and relatively easy-to-use Web browser technology.

The Internet standards have created a universal network into which every company and human being and company in the world can be connected

It's interesting that you single out your Office suite as your "power tools," since these products are currently all wired with Internet technology!

While you are working in Microsoft Word, did you know that your program can actually simultaneously check online resources on the Internet? Or that you can embed real-time stock quote queries into an Excel spreadsheet?

This is just one example that points how much the Internet and "on-line" are with us—and are here to stay.

I sometimes prefer to say "online" instead of "Internet" because the new millennium will bring us new options in networking. The Internet may eventually become the over-, under-, or outernet.

But it will remain a collection of networks connected through common "languages" that enable computing devices to communicate with each other, regardless of operating system, microprocessor, or user interface. The network will become ubiquitous to users, very much like public utilities: water, gas, and electricity.

When was the last time you thought about nuclear reactors or the Hoover Dam when you flipped on a light switch? Do you think about the intricate network of pipes, canals, tunnels, and other waterways when you turn on the tap for a cool glass of water? Probably not.

Yet these are examples of professionally managed, well-maintained networks that deliver vital services to your home and office. And you, as a user, determine when, how much, and for what purpose you want to use the water, gas, and electricity.

And everybody is plugged in because, on the Internet, everybody's computer can communicate with millions of computers all over the world using a universal communications protocol called TCP/IP. This protocol, developed by the military/academic complex in the 1960s lets all computers, regardless of make, model, or operating system, talk with each other. It made the Internet revolution happen.

That is the technology that created the Internet revolution. And it can also make things easier—and cheaper—in your company, Eric.

You can today use the Internet to exchange information easily with customers, prospects, competitors, suppliers, and complete strangers anywhere in the world

But with your conventional computer system you can't look into your own customer database which is housed 100 feet from your office. Installing a simple Intranet can make your customer information more readily available to you—and anyone else in your company who needs it.

An Internet Web site has a "three-tiered architecture."

1. *Web Server:* This can be a sturdy PC or larger computer that receives and sends messages from your Web site.
2. *Middleware Application:* This does all the real work.

Figure III.7

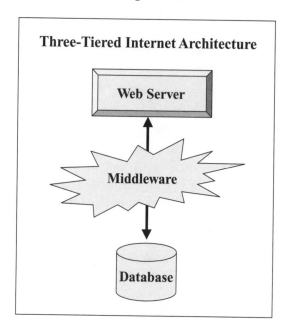

3. *Customer Database:* This is a giant Rolodex constantly being added to with information and insights gained from the middleware application.

Figure III.7 shows an example of such an infrastructure.

Usually you do not need to replace all your hardware. Mainframes and other legacy systems can now easily be modified to provide or connect to Internet protocols and technologies.

The three-tiered architecture is typical of all interactive installations, big or small.

- *The Web Server* is the computer that physically handles the communications between a user and his Web browser, such as Netscape, and any data being requested that it has access to. The Web server has no knowledge of your customer database or what to do with the information stored on it.
- *The Middleware Application* is a set of programs, most freely available and ready out of the box, that understand how to interpret a request sent from the Web server for storing or retrieving data from your database.

- *The Database* is the store of information and data about your company, products, people, etc. and your customers, whether or not they visit your Web site.

Let's see how this works:

One of your customers—let's say this Struckman guy—logs on to your customer Web site (with a protected password log-in) and requests the status of his latest order.

The middleware (aptly named since it sits in the middle of the Web and database servers) looks at the request and translates that into code, or a language that your database understands. The database processes the request and sends the information back to the middleware application, which in turn hands it off to the web server to transform the data into a nicely formatted "page" of information that Struckman sees via his Netscape or Explorer Web browser.

The middleware layer can also be programmed to perform a plethora of nifty tasks based on "rule sets" that can be programmed into its business logic.

Your Web site, Eric, can have functionality programmed into it to evaluate requests and perform additional tasks and provide additional information. Remember that an actual living, breathing customer is interacting with you, so you want to take maximum advantage of your time with that customer!

Let's say Struckman has been checking his order status twice a day. Your middleware application business logic could easily be programmed to catch this pattern and provide the order status with an additional message: "Would you like Mildred Fudd to call you right now to explain the status of your order?"

Simultaneously a message could be sent to Mildred with all the details about Struckman's orders, his tracking history, contact information, complaints, etc.

I am particularly proud of the Intelligent Web Server (IWS) we helped put together for IBM.

This server identified where a site visitor came from: a particular banner, a "micro-site," or even a search engine.

If a visitor came from a search on Yahoo looking for better financial software, we assumed that this was a financial person—perhaps a CFO—and dynamically presented a page layout and copy that was targeted to financial folks.

We also made available a special "kit" that explained the technical benefits of the system, which the financial visitor could send immediately to his counterpart in IT and to other members of the decision-making units.

Profiling technology and protocols generate highly valuable information on your customers and prospects.

Customer and prospect profiling normally takes place during a "session," the period of time that a customer is using your interactive interface. Almost every move your customer or prospect makes can be tracked, providing smart marketers with raw knowledge of their customers' behavior.

For instance, Eric, one of your customers—maybe SpeedServ—always buys the inexpensive Widget A. But the middleware sees that he also looks at the spec sheet of the more expensive Widget B.

You can start making some assumptions based on this behavior and make him an offer he can't refuse: B Widgets at a special price for a try-out period of one month.

Even a "brochure ware" Web site—one that allows only for consumption of corporate information and no feedback or interactive options—can collect relevant information about the people (customers and prospects) who are visiting your site.

These clues are left mainly in your Web site's server in the form of a log. You can cull relevant data from a Web server's log file and interpret that data into marketing information.

But you first have to understand the basics of communications on the Internet.

The key concept is copying. That's right—almost every action performed on the Internet is simply copying a file (just like a word processing file) from a server (or host) computer to the computer of the Web site visitor.

The actual copying of files that make up pages is seamless. One mouse click instructs the server computer to send a copy of that page (file) to the visitor and display it in the proper formatting with the help of his or her browser (usually Netscape or Internet Explorer).

In retrieving the desired information, the visitor also leaves some important clues on the server, which show up in what is commonly called the "server log."

Look at this example which could be yours at InterTech, Eric:

ed.hq.iweb.net—[14/Jan/1999:13:03:30 -0500] "GET/index.html
   HTTP/1.0" 200 2894
ed.hq.iweb.net—[14/Jan/1999:13:03:31 -0500] "GET/images/home.
   jpg HTTP/1.0" 200 1493
ed.hq.iweb.net—[14/Jan/1999:13:03:32 -0500] "GET/images/crosshair.
   jpg HTTP/1.0" 200 2283
ed.hq.iweb.net—[14/Jan/1999:13:03:52 -0500] "GET/Content/Products/
   technology.html"

Each line shows a file being transferred from the server to the visitor's computer and reveals this information:

- the name of the visitor's computer—*ed.hq.iweb.net*
- followed by the date and time of the activity—*[14/Jan/1999: 13:03:30 -0500*
- a command to copy a file to the visitor's computer—*GET/ index.html HTTP/1.0"*
- and some coded statistics about the success of the copy and the file size—*200 2894*

Each of these lines is called a "hit" to your server; hence the name "hits." Hits are significant in many aspects. But just counting all your hits doesn't tell us how successful your site is—it merely tells you how many files were transferred.

The first two hits on the files, *index.html* and *home.jpg,* called up the words, pictures, and formatting that make up this Web site's home page. No exciting news.

But then the visitor calls for the file *"GET/Content/Products/technology.html."* This tells us that visitor *ed.hq.iweb.net* clearly is interested in your technology and products because he or she went straight from your home page to the technology section.

If we follow your prospect further, you may see a path from technology to your sales page, where you have your price lists, terms, and conditions, a signal that your prospect is ready to buy. Your server can then send an e-mail to Joe Epstein signaling that someone online is literally waiting to be pulled over the purchase line.

This powerful profiling technology does data registration and analysis, automated and in real time. No expensive and time-consuming customer interview—the Web site does the interviewing!

While all of this may seem incredibly sophisticated and complex, these solutions are now readily available in "off-the-shelf" packages for as little as $5,000.

You can also do some lower-level profiling by examining an aggregated report of your Web site's server logs and start to make assumptions. Your IT department can run these reports for you with several programs available on the Internet today, free or at low cost ($99), such as WebTrends, that provide output in Microsoft Word or Excel format.

Eric: OK, I understand about the profiling, but do we know the identify of ed.hq.iweb.net?

Adam:

Good question! You know the true identity of Web site visitors only if they have registered with you, providing their true name and other information. In other words, you are high on their permission pyramid.

There is a movement afoot called Open Profile Standard (OPS), whereby individuals will have a Personal Profile that contains their personal information.

The first time that an individual visits a Web site that supports OPS, the Web site will request information from the Personal Profile. The individual has the choice of releasing all, some, or none of the requested information to the Web site. In addition, if the Web site collects additional information about the individual's preferences, it can (with the individual's permission) store that information in the Personal Profile for future use. On subsequent visits the individual can authorize the Web site to retrieve the same personal information without asking permission each time.

Only time will tell if OPS becomes a true standard.

Eric: For which kind of business is the Internet more important—companies that sell to consumers or companies, such as ours, that sell to other businesses?

Jay:

Most of the publicity and buzz about the Internet today is about consumer sites—Amazon, Ebay, etc.—and their stock prices. But the real volume of e-commerce is taking place among businesses that are in-volved with each other in the supply chain.

You sell components to makers of dishwashers. Your customers make the product and sell it to wholesalers and retailers, which in turn sell to the consumer. Fairly simple. But think of all the hundreds of companies you deal with—suppliers, travel agents, insurance agents, accountants, the IRS, banks, etc. And the appliance makers you sell to have thousands of suppliers and relations with whom they commu-nicate even before they start talking to their customers.

The bottom line: Business-to-business Internet communications and transactions will be tremendous—according to International Data Research, from $32 billion in 1998 to $425 billion in the year 2002. *And 75% of that growth will come from companies doing business with other companies.*

Adam:

Ninteen ninety-eight and early '99 brought a tremendous rush of "e" words: e-commerce, e-tools, e-technology, e-services, e-everything.

Interestingly enough, business has been using an "e" word for over a decade: EDI, or Electronic Data Interchange.

EDI was truly one of the first e-technologies used in business com-munications, typically between supplier and customers. EDI was a standard, a format if you will, that was mutually agreed upon by in-dustry, for companies and computers to communicate with one another.

The EDI protocol established common formats for transmitting in-formation about orders, pricing, discounts, availability, and order status.

The problem with EDI was cost. Mainframes, back-end processes, and maintenance staffing were needed to participate in the EDI supply chain, prohibiting small and midsized companies from entering the system.

Thanks to freely available ubiquitous client software (Web browsers), smaller, faster servers, and global connectivity through the Internet, the technology barrier to entry has been significantly lowered for all business.

"Gateways" enabled connections to back-office systems, such as mainframes, and put a friendly face on the data, as well as provided greatly simplified command sets and instructions through the Web in-terface. Now any company can provide the same functionality to its cus-tomers as with EDI but without the cost and without most of the hassle.

A famous example of e-commerce at work is Cisco Systems, providers of routers, hubs, and other networking equipment.

Cisco told all their customers they were turning off their EDI interfaces and would take orders only through their freshly launched Web site. This started the move of business-to-business e-commerce through a new, more cost-effective channel.

Today many successful examples of this type of e-business are in the marketplace. Dell Computers jumped to a leadership position by connecting their entire supply chain to their Web site, effectively eliminating the middlemen and intermediaries and migrating to a "build-to-order" business model.

High-tech companies were quick to embrace the new model, since most of their customers were members of the connected economy by the very nature of their business. But not every company has "got religion." In 1998, 90% of all Fortune 500 companies had at the very least a corporate "brochure-ware" Web site. But fewer than 25% of those had actually used any of the available and captured data from customers through those interfaces.

Eric: I've got a going business with great salespeople in the field. If e-commerce means we will be dealing directly and electronically with our customers, what will happen to these guys—and the inside salespeople who back them up?

Jay:
I am willing to bet that your field sales force has more job security in this Internet age than anybody else in your company—except you, of course.

First of all, the Internet is a terrific tool for field salespeople. Your Web site can provide Joe Epstein and the other account managers with a continually updated brochure, catalog, and price list. No more fumbling and mumbling. Plus you can put "sizing tools" on the Web to help your salespeople show the customer which component fits where and how. They can also make complex project calculations on the spot. In short, all the information needed to make the sale is at their fingertips.

Internal communications are also made easier with the Internet. Let's agree that a salesperson must make two sales with every transaction: he or she has to get the order from the customer, then "sell" the order internally to get the stuff delivered. (As I understand it, Eric, you've had some problems in this area.)

In short, the whole problem of customer team communications can be quickly and cheaply fixed with the Internet or an internal Intranet.

Finally, I am convinced that in the business-to-business setting, the salesperson will ultimately be the method and media to drive customers and prospects to your e-commerce Web site. When you add up the thousands of dollars buying buttons, banners, and other online marketing efforts to get people online, you may find out that the $200 cost per visit of a salesperson, equipped with a PC may be more cost-effective.

I mentioned this to someone last year who remarked that Dell Computers was using this model: a salesperson would visit the customer and demonstrate a Web site tailor-made to the customer's situation, based on the profiling data Adam talked about. He then "trained" the customer on how to use this tailor-made, personal Web site to order stuff from Dell.

The result: Something like a zillion dollars per day in extra orders. (Dell also has come a bit late to Customer Marketing!)

Adam:

Any company thinking about opening an online sales channel will have to deal with their current sales channels.

The hardest part is the transition between the two. There are many examples of companies that just didn't have the "guts" to confront their sales force.

Avon was very daring by adopting online sales early on, despite their army of "Avon ladies." Over time it became a win-win situation. Sales increased from existing customers and new customers.

Most important, new opportunities were created for the sales reps because Avon clients were offered two delivery options:

- UPS delivery in two or three days
- A smiling Avon representative (with catalog and samples) to bring the order to their home tomorrow. Bingo!

Traditional sales channels feel threatened by "computers taking over" mainly because they are right! Computers are taking over some routine transactions for "commodity" items, just as the call center took over some routine transactions for "commodity" items.

But the computer can never take over the function of building lasting, personal relationships or solving complex problems. Or taking customers and prospects out to the ballgame.

Jay:

The real job loss in your company, Eric, may be in warehousing and logistics. As your industry moves into e-commerce mode, there will be more "just-in-time" deliveries between makers and users. Hopefully, with firms like InterTech still sitting in between the maker and the buyer.

This gets back to your "business model." What business are you really in?

The continuing dialogue with your customers will show the way, as you know more than most.

Eric: I know, I know: getting customers, keeping customers, and maximizing customer profitability.

Adam:

Right on!

Eric: What should be my role as CEO in getting our Internet operation up and running?

Jay:

Change never happens without top-down commitment. And the Internet will mean change. What should Eric be doing here, Adam?

Adam:

The simplest way to show that you as leader are a part of and committed to the change is to actively participate in it.

- Use e-mail.
- Surf the Web every day and pass along to your employees interesting Web sites that you have found, relevant news articles, or other sources that will enable competitive advantage.
- Study the daily statistics on "hit rates," leads, and orders generated by your Web site.

You would be amazed at the number of CEOs in the U.S. who have their assistants print out their e-mail, to be commented on, marked up, and returned for the assistants to eventually send responses. But getting online is only a starting point.

The toughest part of implementing e-commerce into any established business is addressing the internal "FUD" factors—Fear, Uncertainty, and Doubt.

The only way to alleviate employee FUD is to involve them in the process from day one. Present the mission, show how it may affect their lives short- and long-term, and hold steady to your mission.

The best way to involve these people and departments is to educate them as much as possible.

And you, Eric, the CEO, should stand by their side in training sessions and open discussions. This will let you speak intelligently about the change, give you a much better understanding of the issues they will be facing, and measure personally the progress the company is making in the change to a digital future.

Your IT staff may be especially upset about the Internet. Will their jobs be taken by outside consultants with E-xperience? Are their direction and initiatives clear to them? Most important, sales/marketing and IT are separated by culture and language. That's what most of the "Dilbert" comic strip is all about.

Most of my time at Think New Ideas, Inc., was spent working with large companies' internal IT and marketing groups, helping them understand each other's language, challenges, and issues, as well as the fact that they will never live separate from each other again.

Eric: In other words, we have to include IT in the customer teams . . .

Adam and Jay (in unison):
Exactly!

Eric: We have an Internet site, of course. But I guess it's what you would call an "electronic brochure," which my nephew put together. I guess we need to turn it into an e-commerce site. What are the specific steps involved in setting up our Internet presence?

Jay:
Adam, what's the good news and the bad news on this?

Adam:

First, the good news: The fact that you have an existing Web site means you have gotten over the initial barrier to entry hurdles, such as domain name, initial hardware and software configurations, etc.

I took a good look at your Web site, Eric, and your nephew is not a bad Web designer.

Next, the bad news: You will need to complete these steps:

1. Decide how you want to use interactive technologies in your business.
2. Conduct an internal evaluation of existing systems and resources.
3. Conduct an external competitive audit about what your competitors, "the other guys," are doing.
4. Make a blueprint of the types of processes you wish to create or existing processes you wish to "enable."
5. Make a "style guide" for both content and look and feel. Remember that the written word on your Web site is as important as how you speak in any external communications, through TV, radio, print, or otherwise.
6. Establish a budget, both for time and cost, with a budget for your own time and/or that of a project manager.

Eric: But that checklist looks the same as what the IT analysts, programmers, and consultants use.

Adam:

You've got it, Eric. Because setting up a full-blown e-commerce operation is equivalent to re-engineering most, if not all, of your IT infrastructure, with an impact on all departments: production, logistics, and administration, as shown in Figure III.8 (which may seem familiar to you).

I am sure that your nephew is a very capable and talented bright young man. But would you hire him to redesign the IT architecture of InterTech?

But there is some good news in all of this: you can have a fully functional system up and running within 6 to 12 weeks after attending the last boring project meeting.

And at a cost of about 35% to 40% of what you are used to paying

Figure III.8

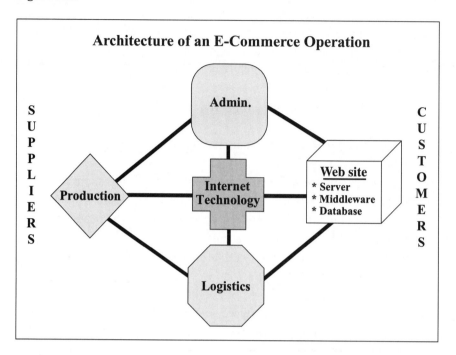

the systems guys to put something together.

This is possible because you can work with free or inexpensive applications. And with the Internet protocols you can normally get the boxes to communicate with each other with less hassle.

Eric: Should we set up an e-commerce operation ourselves or hire a company to do it for us?

Adam:
The choice is not a digital this or that. Success comes from combining the best of your internal and external resources.

Of course, there are many firms that will gladly take your money and create all strategies and implementation for you. But you will wind up with much less of the knowledge in-house that went into the project. And you will have a tough time getting buy-in from all groups in your organization.

This statement sounds somewhat harsh toward the interactive architect services sector. These firms—such as the company I started—are very useful partners for large companies, which all suffer from being big, smart, and slow. Today's connected economy calls for nimble operations with a business plan that allows for "moving targets."

But I can safely say that you will require the help of "the big guns" only if you choose not to be an active participant in the process. Most of the large firm consulting hours you pay for on your e-commerce implementation are spent tracking down assets and holding countless policy and steering committee meetings that are all about the strategy you wish to implement and very little about the implementation itself.

A seasoned IT department can complete a full e-commerce initiative with few additional resources. But you MUST make those few available or risk total meltdown and failure.

One resource you need is *design*. Technologists are usually lousy designers, so you will need parallel development expertise to design the "look and feel" of your e-commerce site. The interface with the outside world is critical because it projects your "virtual brand," which should not clash with your existing branding and marketing materials. And the way your Web site interacts with the visitors should also be consistent with the image you want to project.

If you think your nephew understands your brand and image, there is no need to fire him—put him on your e-commerce development team.

But you and your nephew must have—on the payroll or on contract—a good programmer/analyst familiar with the Internet.

Programmers come in many shapes and sizes. But you would be amazed at how normal they are!

I have employed hundreds of programmers and can assure you their image as Jolt-cola-drinking, penguin-logo-T-shirt wearing, skateboard-to-work-riding people is just as accurate as the greedy yuppie MBA stereotype.

Showing interest in the human capital of your programmer will result in a reciprocal effect. Your goal is not to understand the technology but to inspire your programmer(s) to take interest in the business process problem you are seeking to solve and become a recognized stakeholder in the project.

Asking him or her for an inventory of your e-business capabilities is the perfect way to start this project. Staying *personally involved* with the programmers doing the actual work not only will be an amazing inspiration to the work force but will leave you amazed at how much of this stuff you can learn just by observing. You will not be sorry for spending the effort understanding in concept how these pieces work, especially when you are considering bringing in outside consultants, design specialists, and other interactive architecture firms.

Eric: Where should we have the hardware installation for our e-commerce operation? In-house or outside?

Adam:

Your server can be on premises. But many companies are now outsourcing the hardware side to professional data centers that provide year-round monitoring of your system's "health" and guarantees on uptime of the network connection, power supply, and physical security.

These services can be useful, but I strongly advise you ALWAYS to keep the systems management in-house. This will save you lots of hassles later when it is time to upgrade your systems, procedures, or e-enabling technologies. You really want to keep this knowledge in-house and well documented.

You should also make sure that you have in-house a good set of "update tools." These tools enable you or any other nontechnical person to update information in selected areas of your site. There is absolutely no reason to hire someone else to do this for you at additional cost.

You yourself should be able to update the InterTech Web site with the weekly "Letter from the CEO" that you publish directly from your laptop for all the world to see.

Of course, if you wish to do a major overhaul or change the underlying process you put in place, you will need to bring in the pros.

One company that has an optimal mix of inside and outside resources is The Gap. This San Francisco–based clothing company already does its marketing, advertising, and e-commerce in-house. IT is truly a member of the Customer Team.

But The Gap does use a few external consultants when needed to supplement their internal IT and marketing knowledge. My company has provided them with external media-buying services and competitive research at times. But I have always been very impressed with the scale of that company's knowledge, which has resulted in extraordinary market and mind share.

Eric: I've been reading all these stories about companies like Amazon started from scratch by a handful of nerds and now millions of people all over the world buying stuff from them. Once we get our new Internet site up and running for our current customers, how can we "go global" and get companies all over the world to visit it and start their journey up our customer pyramid?

Adam:

First let's look at the "successful nerd" business model.

Successes such as Amazon.com and Yahoo came from a new hybrid breed: the wired businessperson. Throughout the past 30 years business has had three basic areas of internal resources: the business process group, the marketing group, and the information systems group.

In today's business and forevermore, marketing and technology must be completely integrated. Universities have been literal petri dishes for cultivating programmers with enough marketing training and access to free software (Open Source) and powerful computing resources to create the very businesses that hold billion-dollar market capitalization today.

The actual technology behind Amazon, Yahoo, Ebay, or any other high-flying tech company is nothing you can't put together for a couple of thousand dollars.

Scale of their businesses is the key, which in turn requires more computing resources.

But the basic technology is completely available to anyone interested in putting the right pieces together. Since you are not a computer programmer, you will have to learn how to find the right people to assist you with your interactive marketing blueprint. So the first step, Eric, is to get your act together internally! But we have talked about that already.

Creating a Web site, whether it's interactive or brochure-ware, does not ensure that your "virtual shingle" will drive customers to your system/site. There are many ways to ensure exposure and as many ways to do this correctly (or not!).

Setting up a Web site and not telling anyone about it or how to get to it is equivalent to creating a nice neon sign with your company logo on it and throwing it into the Atlantic Ocean.

Common sense and proven interactive marketing techniques will get your suspects to your site quickly if you follow these steps:

What's in a name?

Yourname.com, if chosen correctly and available, will increase the percentage of people searching for your product. If you sell Widgets, you would, of course, want to register a domain name widgets.com.

Domain names are the human-language equivalent of server names. Servers identify themselves with a numeric scheme, each unique to all servers and computers on the Internet. Your server may have the "address" 198.187.36.44, which isn't as easy to remember as widgets.com.

The problem is that most category names, like *widgets, cars, books,* or *music,* are already registered, so you will have to come up with a smart variation, or understand how to brand your domain name. Who ever thought *Amazon* would become synonymous with *books?*

Online marketing

Registering your domain name, company name, and the type of product or service you are providing with the top "search engines" is your next stop.

Every top search engine, such as Yahoo, Excite, or Lycos, will allow you to do this at no charge, and there are several Web sites that allow you to enter your information once and will automatically upload it to all the leading search engines for you, providing a detailed report when complete.

This will greatly enhance the chance that suspects looking for you or your type of product will find your domain name and visit your site.

A side note here: Most search engines now sell "key word" exclusivity. You can actually negotiate with these companies to put your "link" at the top of the results list if searched on certain key words you specify. This will ensure that the top link in a search for widgets will be a link to your Web site. This can become quite costly, depending on your direct competition and the ambiguity of the key word. You may be surprised to hear that IBM for many years has "owned" the key word *Windows* instead of Microsoft!

Banners are another method for online marketing to get suspects to come to your site. A banner is like a mini ad, displayed usually at the top of a Web site. Banner messaging and placement works very much like traditional advertising. There are many services and companies that will place your banners on Web sites and other online places that will attract the type of user with the characteristics you desire. When clicked on, the banner will transport your suspect to your Web site. This DOESN'T have to be your home page, or front door, by the way.

You may decide to make a different "entrance" to your information for a user who clicks on a banner showing your most expensive widget rather than a banner showing your cheapest. This can also be programmed into your middleware application logic to change your messaging dynamically based on banner click, key words used at a search engine, or even if suspects didn't come from an online link at all but typed your domain directly into their browser because they saw an ad in some form of traditional media.

Offline marketing

Traditional marketing methods and a "shotgun blast" approach are still extremely effective for getting visitors to your Web site. Again, your domain name is important here. Words that are easily remembered and contain conventional spelling will work best in this scenario. In general, less is more.

Tagging television, radio, and print with your URL (common-speak for your domain name) and printing it on your packaging and collateral material entail little cost with high returns.

And, as Jay has mentioned, your field and telesales people may be the most effective ways to get customers and prospects to be regular e-commerce buyers.

Registration and identification

When a suspect, prospect, or even an existing customer comes to your interactive interface, there is no failsafe way to know who that person is. We can, however, program our middleware application to be able to identify if that particular computer the visitor is using has been to your site before. This is done by giving your visitor's browser program a small, nonintrusive ID tag.

Known as a "cookie" (a typical nonsensical geek name), it can contain information relevant to your site only. So we can give each unidentified visitor a cookie to identify a return visit and track his or her session, but we would really want to put a face and name to the computer we identify. This is done through what is commonly known as registration.

Experience shows that visitors are happy to give you their confidential information, such as name, e-mail address, and geographic location, if you follow these two "permission" rules.

- Create and make a complete privacy statement available. This statement will explain what you will and won't do with the visitor's information.
- Show a benefit you will give to any visitor who registers (a free special report on the home appliance market in the next five years!) to your registering visitor. A reward, no matter how small, goes a long way!

One final note: Going "global," as you put it, requires more than just technology and infrastructure. To go global you need local knowledge, just as you do in the "offline world."

Design, language, and culture are key for your global step. The technology will certainly enable the global connection to prospects, even if you don't want them as customers. The Internet is global by nature. But if you want global customers, simply translating your message into other languages is not enough. You need to *localize* your Web site to key language/cultural segments.

A poorly managed localization process can cost you a lot of money and goodwill. We did some research for a networking client, and I was astounded to discover that using the color red was deemed very offensive in certain countries. And the translations included some horrible grammatical errors that completely turned off all site visitors.

Eric: I guess I have to start building my global e-commerce presence by calling Bob Struckman to get him and my other customers online. After that, who knows. . . .

Anyway, thanks for giving me some of your time.

Adam:
You're quite welcome—I enjoyed the experience.

Jay:
Keep in touch, Eric, to let us know how things turn out.

Epilogue

To: jay@curry.com, adam@curry.com
From: eric.dines@intertech.com
Subject: InterTech developments

Jay, Adam:

I promised to let you know what happened at InterTech after our chat some time ago.

First let me fill you in on the Customer Marketing "model project" at our Midwest division,

I will give you the results by using the numbers on customer performance: customer satisfaction, customer behavior, and customer value.

Customer Satisfaction Results

We had some problems with our "back office" value propositions, especially delivery times. But our Speedy Service Group, led by Vincent Brown, tackled the problems with rigor. We did a recent satisfaction measurement on these value propositions. All of the scores—including delivery times—are now 4.0 or above. The "Value for Money" score is still under 4.0, but we did move it up a bit, primarily, we believe, because our service has improved (see Figure III.9).

Customer Behavior Results

As you can see from the "migration matrix" and customer pyramid covering the last 12 months, we realized a 2% net customer loss—and a 14% net gain in revenues!

We lost some larger customers to Internet-based competition, but

Figure III.9

InterTech Customer Satisfaction Results

Scores	Before	After
Delivery times	3.3	**4.0**
Price/value for money	3.8	3.9
Meet agreements and deadlines	3.9	**4.2**
Speed of technical service	3.9	**4.1**

we were able to compensate this with upgrading some Medium and Small customers to Top status. And, of course, we kept the great majority of our customers in their pyramid at the same spending (see Figure III.10).

You may be interested to know how the customer team fared with the selection of customers they were working with (see Figure III.11).

Some customers performed according to plan, others not. But the result was 18% above target, and that's good enough to convince me that the customer team approach works!

Figure III.10

InterTech Customer Behavior Results: Customer Base

	Begin CM	Top	Big	Medium	Small	Inactive	Prospects	Suspects
Top	4	3	1					
Big	18	0	9	2	5	2		
Medium	68	2	4	39	19	2		
Small	360	1	1	19 -	295	44		
Inactive	99	0	3	2	8	86		
Prospects	37	0	1	3	9	0	24	
Suspects	380	0	0	0	17	0	12	351
Customer Results	443	6	19	65	353			

Difference Customers	−7	2	1	−3	−7	35	−1	−29
Difference Revenues	$275,758	283,057	25,698	−24,293	−8,705			
Difference Customers %	−2%							
Difference Revenues%	14%							

Figure III.11

InterTech Customer Behavior Results: Customer Selection

Customer Name	Target Revenue	Revenue Realized	Variance vs. Target
Struckman	$300,000	$354,647	18%
Boards Unlimited	150,000	134,098	−11%
Silicon Sync	100,000	98,403	−2%
Green Machine	30,000	57,648	92%
SpeedServ	35,000	76,298	118%
Main	1,000	0	−100%
Sentinel Service	6,000	5,478	−9%
Colby Corp.	14,000	12,849	−8%
Bates Milling	3,500	7,638	118%
Montpelier SA	2,000	3,728	86%
de Vries Inc.	0	0	0
Bristol	6,000	19,283	221%
Wilkes Corp.	0	0	0
Jones & Long	7,500	0	−100%
British Techno	4,000	7,382	85%
Cellular Tel	0	0	0
Bowdoin Bros.	0	0	0
Total	**$659,000**	**$777,452**	**18%**

Customer Value Results

What was the impact of Customer Marketing on the bottom line? I can't complain—an 85% jump in profits (see Figure III.12).

But I knew this was the last year we could show any profit growth without some kind of e-commerce operation.

We managed to keep the Struckman business—just. But the defection of two Big and two Medium customers to Internet-based suppliers was a very clear message for me: get on the Net or die!

Figure III.12

InterTech Results Last Year			InterTech Customer Value Results		Change $	Change %
Revenues	$2,026,983	100%	Revenues	$2,302,701	$275,758	14%
Direct Costs	1,183,484	58%	Direct Costs	1,358,594	175,110	15%
Margin %	42%		Margin %	41%	0	−1%
Margin	843,499	42%	Margin	944,107	106,608	12%
General Overheads	355,000	18%	General Overheads	365,650	10,650	3%
Profit before M&S	488,499	24%	Profit before M&S	578,457	89,958	18%
Marketing & Sales			Marketing & Sales			
Sales Costs	302,000	15%	Sales Costs	311,060	9,060	3%
Marketing Costs	25,000	1%	Marketing Costs	25,750	750	3%
M&S Overheads	70,000	3%	M&S Overheads	72,100	2,100	3%
Total M&S Costs	397,000	20%	Total M&S Costs	408,910	11,910	3%
Operational Profit	$91,499	5%	Operational Profit	$169,547	$78,048	85%
Customers	450		Customers	443	−7	−2%
Revenue per Customer	$4,504		Revenue per Customer	$5,198	694	15%
Profit per Customer	$203		Profit per Customer	383	179	88%
ROI on M&S	23%		ROI on M&S	41%	18%	80%

Internet Developments

The numbers I have just given you do not reflect any of our Internet activities. The books closed just about the time we got our e-commerce site up and running. Go check it out: *www.widgetsnet.com.*

Here's what happened.

After our meeting with you guys, I immediately did some more analysis of the question about the Internet on the customer interview questionnaire (I admit we hadn't really looked hard at that data!). It became quite clear that most of our customers wanted to do business on the Internet—but most of them were not yet ready for it internally.

Then I got on the telephone and called some Widget makers all over the world with whom we have been in touch—but never done any business because of the distance problem. In no time I got nonexclusive distribution agreements valid if the transactions were handled in "cyberspace."

We immediately called a meeting with Bob Struckman and some of

Figure III.13

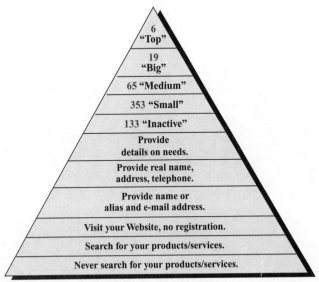

The InterTech Customer Pyramid:
Prior to Launch of E-Commerce Operations

our larger customers and put it to them: "We are going to offer you ordering services via the Internet. And we want to build this system working with you to make sure it meets your needs—not only for ordering our products but also to give you up-to-date information on Widget supplies and suppliers all over the world."

They agreed the idea was pretty good, so I hired a great programmer, Sebastian Neucel, and put him together with my nephew to talk with these customers and our internal people. They came up with a plan and design for orders plus the database of price lists and news from the worldwide Widget suppliers.

We figured speed and functionality were more important than beautiful, so after about eight weeks we were up and running.

What was the result? Look at the customer pyramid at the end of the year—just before we got started (see Figure III.13).

Then look at what it is now, after just 90 days of operation—25 new customers, some of them big ones (see Figure III.14). We even got some customers from Europe and Asia!

Figure III.14

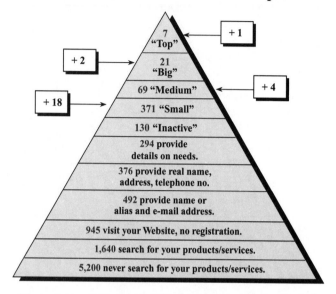

The InterTech Customer Pyramid: 90 Days after Launch of E-Commerce Operations

Pretty much all of our pre-Internet customers have stayed with us. It all seems too good to be true. But you have to trust me on that.

Best regards,
Eric Dines
eric.dines@intertech.com
www.widgetsnet.com

Appendixes

Appendix A.
InterTech Customer Sort

Guideline

Column A: Customer Number
A unique customer number is useful if some customers have the same or similar corporate names.

Column B: Customer Rank
Useful information—but also needed to count up the number of active customers so that percentages can be calculated.

Column C: Customer Name
This is an excellent opportunity to correct spelling errors in customer names!

Column D: Last Year Revenues
This can be some other set period than a year. And "Revenues" can be some other behavior variable, such as number volumes of purchases.

Column E: Cumulative Revenues
The cumulative revenues are added up as each customer joins the list. The last line in this column will equal all revenues in the period. The only function of this column is to help you set your pyramid levels.

Column F: Percent of Customers
This is calculated by dividing the cumulative number of customers by the total number of customers.

Column G: Percent of Revenues
This is calculated by dividing the cumulative revenues by the total revenues.

A	B	C	D	E	F	G	H
		InterTech Customer Sort					
Customer Number	**Cust. Rank**	**Customer Name**	**Last Year Revenues**	**Cum. Revenues**	**Percent of Customers**	**Percent of Revenues**	**Pyramid Levels**
11163	1	Name of Customer	296,337	296,337	0.22%	14.62%	
11138	2	Name of Customer	143,945	440,282	0.44%	21.72%	**Top 1%**
11113	3	Name of Customer	74,896	515,178	0.67%	25.42%	
11064	4	Name of Customer	50,937	566,115	0.89%	27.93%	
11039	5	Name of Customer	49,935	616,050	1.11%	30.39%	
11014	6	Name of Customer	46,150	662,200	1.33%	32.67%	
10965	7	Name of Customer	42,365	704,565	1.56%	34.76%	
10940	8	Name of Customer	38,580	743,145	1.78%	36.66%	
10915	9	Name of Customer	33,062	776,207	2.00%	38.29%	
10866	10	Name of Customer	31,010	807,217	2.22%	39.82%	
10841	11	Name of Customer	27,225	834,442	2.44%	41.17%	
10816	12	Name of Customer	25,440	859,882	2.67%	42.42%	
10767	13	Name of Customer	23,691	883,573	2.89%	43.59%	**Big 4%**
10742	14	Name of Customer	18,670	902,243	3.11%	44.51%	
10717	15	Name of Customer	17,985	920,228	3.33%	45.40%	
10668	16	Name of Customer	17,300	937,528	3.56%	46.25%	
11188	17	Name of Customer	16,615	954,143	3.78%	47.07%	
11164	18	Name of Customer	15,930	970,073	4.00%	47.86%	
11139	19	Name of Customer	15,245	985,318	4.22%	48.61%	
11114	20	Name of Customer	14,560	999,878	4.44%	49.33%	
11089	21	Name of Customer	14,476	1,014,354	4.67%	50.04%	
11065	22	Name of Customer	14,322	1,028,676	4.89%	50.75%	
11040	23	Name of Customer	14,317	1,042,993	5.11%	51.46%	
11015	24	Name of Customer	14,081	1,057,074	5.33%	52.15%	
10990	25	Name of Customer	13,870	1,070,944	5.56%	52.83%	
10966	26	Name of Customer	13,659	1,084,603	5.78%	53.51%	
10941	27	Name of Customer	13,448	1,098,051	6.00%	54.17%	
10916	28	Name of Customer	13,237	1,111,288	6.22%	54.82%	
10891	29	Name of Customer	13,026	1,124,314	6.44%	55.47%	
10867	30	Name of Customer	12,815	1,137,129	6.67%	56.10%	
10842	31	Name of Customer	12,604	1,149,733	6.89%	56.72%	
10817	32	Name of Customer	12,393	1,162,126	7.11%	57.33%	
10792	33	Name of Customer	12,182	1,174,308	7.33%	57.93%	
10768	34	Name of Customer	11,971	1,186,279	7.56%	58.52%	
10743	35	Name of Customer	11,760	1,198,039	7.78%	59.10%	
10718	36	Name of Customer	11,549	1,209,588	8.00%	59.67%	
10693	37	Name of Customer	11,338	1,220,926	8.22%	60.23%	
10669	38	Name of Customer	11,127	1,232,053	8.44%	60.78%	
11189	39	Name of Customer	10,921	1,242,974	8.67%	61.32%	
11165	40	Name of Customer	10,715	1,253,689	8.89%	61.85%	
11140	41	Name of Customer	10,509	1,264,198	9.11%	62.37%	
11115	42	Name of Customer	10,303	1,274,501	9.33%	62.88%	**Medium 15%**
11090	43	Name of Customer	10,097	1,284,598	9.56%	63.37%	
11066	44	Name of Customer	9,891	1,294,489	9.78%	63.86%	
11041	45	Name of Customer	9,685	1,304,174	10.00%	64.34%	
11016	46	Name of Customer	9,479	1,313,653	10.22%	64.81%	
10991	47	Name of Customer	9,273	1,322,926	10.44%	65.27%	
10967	48	Name of Customer	9,067	1,331,993	10.67%	65.71%	
10942	49	Name of Customer	8,861	1,340,854	10.89%	66.15%	
10917	50	Name of Customer	8,655	1,349,509	11.11%	66.58%	
10892	51	Name of Customer	8,449	1,357,958	11.33%	66.99%	
10868	52	Name of Customer	8,243	1,366,201	11.56%	67.40%	
10843	53	Name of Customer	8,037	1,374,238	11.78%	67.80%	
10818	54	Name of Customer	7,831	1,382,069	12.00%	68.18%	
10793	55	Name of Customer	7,625	1,389,694	12.22%	68.56%	
10769	56	Name of Customer	7,419	1,397,113	12.44%	68.93%	
10744	57	Name of Customer	7,213	1,404,326	12.67%	69.28%	
10719	58	Name of Customer	7,007	1,411,333	12.89%	69.63%	
10694	59	Name of Customer	6,801	1,418,134	13.11%	69.96%	
10670	60	Name of Customer	6,595	1,424,729	13.33%	70.29%	
11190	61	Name of Customer	6,389	1,431,118	13.56%	70.60%	
11166	62	Name of Customer	6,183	1,437,301	13.78%	70.91%	

(continued)

A	B	C	D	E	F	G	H
InterTech Customer Sort (continued)							
Customer Number	Cust. Rank	Customer Name	Last Year Revenues	Cum. Revenues	Percent of Customers	Percent of Revenues	Pyramid Levels
11141	63	Name of Customer	5,977	1,443,278	14.00%	71.20%	
11116	64	Name of Customer	5,771	1,449,049	14.22%	71.49%	
11091	65	Name of Customer	5,565	1,454,614	14.44%	71.76%	
		Customer List Shortened to Save Space					
10869	74	Name of Customer	5,020	1,500,665	16.44%	74.03%	
10844	75	Name of Customer	5,001	1,505,666	16.67%	74.28%	
10819	76	Name of Customer	4,982	1,510,648	16.89%	74.53%	
10794	77	Name of Customer	4,963	1,515,611	17.11%	74.77%	**Medium**
10770	78	Name of Customer	4,944	1,520,555	17.33%	75.02%	**15%**
10745	79	Name of Customer	4,937	1,525,492	17.56%	75.26%	
10720	80	Name of Customer	4,930	1,530,422	17.78%	75.50%	
10695	81	Name of Customer	4,923	1,535,345	18.00%	75.75%	
10671	82	Name of Customer	4,916	1,540,261	18.22%	75.99%	
11191	83	Name of Customer	4,909	1,545,170	18.44%	76.23%	
11167	84	Name of Customer	4,902	1,550,072	18.67%	76.47%	
11142	85	Name of Customer	4,895	1,554,967	18.89%	76.71%	
11117	86	Name of Customer	4,888	1,559,855	19.11%	76.95%	
11092	87	Name of Customer	4,881	1,564,736	19.33%	77.20%	
11068	88	Name of Customer	4,874	1,569,610	19.56%	77.44%	
11043	89	Name of Customer	4,867	1,574,477	19.78%	77.68%	
11018	90	Name of Customer	4,832	1,579,309	20.00%	77.91%	
10993	91	Name of Customer	4,791	1,584,100	20.22%	78.15%	
10969	92	Name of Customer	4,754	1,588,854	20.44%	78.39%	
10944	93	Name of Customer	4,717	1,593,571	20.67%	78.62%	
10919	94	Name of Customer	4,680	1,598,251	20.89%	78.85%	
10894	95	Name of Customer	4,643	1,602,894	21.11%	79.08%	
10870	96	Name of Customer	4,606	1,607,500	21.33%	79.31%	
10845	97	Name of Customer	4,569	1,612,069	21.56%	79.53%	
10820	98	Name of Customer	4,532	1,616,601	21.78%	79.75%	
10795	99	Name of Customer	4,495	1,621,096	22.00%	79.98%	
10771	100	Name of Customer	4,458	1,625,554	22.22%	80.20%	
10746	101	Name of Customer	4,421	1,629,975	22.44%	80.41%	
10721	102	Name of Customer	4,384	1,634,359	22.67%	80.63%	
10696	103	Name of Customer	4,347	1,638,706	22.89%	80.84%	
10672	104	Name of Customer	4,310	1,643,016	23.11%	81.06%	
11192	105	Name of Customer	4,273	1,647,289	23.33%	81.27%	
11168	106	Name of Customer	4,236	1,651,525	23.56%	81.48%	
11093	107	Name of Customer	4,189	1,655,714	23.78%	81.68%	
11069	108	Name of Customer	4,145	1,659,859	24.00%	81.89%	**Small**
10994	109	Name of Customer	4,099	1,663,958	24.22%	82.09%	**80%**
10970	110	Name of Customer	4,052	1,668,010	24.44%	82.29%	
10895	111	Name of Customer	4,005	1,672,015	24.67%	82.49%	
10871	112	Name of Customer	3,958	1,675,973	24.89%	82.68%	
10796	113	Name of Customer	3,911	1,679,884	25.11%	82.88%	
10772	114	Name of Customer	3,864	1,683,748	25.33%	83.07%	
10697	115	Name of Customer	3,817	1,687,565	25.56%	83.26%	
10673	116	Name of Customer	3,770	1,691,335	25.78%	83.44%	
11193	117	Name of Customer	3,723	1,695,058	26.00%	83.62%	
11169	118	Name of Customer	3,676	1,698,734	26.22%	83.81%	
11143	119	Name of Customer	3,629	1,702,363	26.44%	83.99%	
11118	120	Name of Customer	3,582	1,705,945	26.67%	84.16%	
11094	121	Name of Customer	3,535	1,709,480	26.89%	84.34%	
11070	122	Name of Customer	3,488	1,712,968	27.11%	84.51%	
		Customer List Shortened to Save Space					

A	B	C	D	E	F	G	H
Customer Number	Cust. Rank	Customer Name	Last Year Revenues	Cum. Revenues	Percent of Customers	Percent of Revenues	Pyramid Levels
10885	426	Name of Customer	238	2,021,510	94.67%	99.73%	
10860	427	Name of Customer	238	2,021,748	94.89%	99.74%	
10835	428	Name of Customer	237	2,021,984	95.11%	99.75%	
10810	429	Name of Customer	236	2,022,221	95.33%	99.77%	
10786	430	Name of Customer	236	2,022,457	95.56%	99.78%	
10761	431	Name of Customer	236	2,022,692	95.78%	99.79%	
10736	432	Name of Customer	235	2,022,928	96.00%	99.80%	
10711	433	Name of Customer	234	2,023,162	96.22%	99.81%	
10687	434	Name of Customer	234	2,023,396	96.44%	99.82%	
11207	435	Name of Customer	234	2,023,630	96.67%	99.83%	
11183	436	Name of Customer	233	2,023,862	96.89%	99.85%	
11158	437	Name of Customer	232	2,024,095	97.11%	99.86%	Small
11133	438	Name of Customer	232	2,024,327	97.33%	99.87%	80%
11108	439	Name of Customer	232	2,024,558	97.56%	99.88%	
11084	440	Name of Customer	231	2,024,790	97.78%	99.89%	
11059	441	Name of Customer	230	2,025,020	98.00%	99.90%	
11034	442	Name of Customer	230	2,025,250	98.22%	99.91%	
11009	443	Name of Customer	230	2,025,480	98.44%	99.93%	
10985	444	Name of Customer	229	2,025,709	98.67%	99.94%	
10960	445	Name of Customer	228	2,025,937	98.89%	99.95%	
10935	446	Name of Customer	228	2,026,165	99.11%	99.96%	
10910	447	Name of Customer	228	2,026,392	99.33%	99.97%	
10886	448	Name of Customer	227	2,026,620	99.56%	99.98%	
10861	449	Name of Customer	226	2,026,846	99.78%	99.99%	
10836	450	Name of Customer	137	2,026,983	100.00%	100.00%	
11160	483	Name of Inactive					
11185	482	Name of Inactive					
11209	481	Name of Inactive					
10664	480	Name of Inactive					
		Inactives List Shortened to Save Space					
10713	478	Name of Inactive					Inactives
11211	527	Name of Inactive					
10666	526	Name of Inactive					
10691	525	Name of Inactive					
10715	524	Name of Inactive					
	563	Name of Prospect					
	581	Name of Prospect					
	562	Name of Prospect					
	580	Name of Prospect					
		Prospect List Shortened to Save Space					
	585	Name of Prospect					
	570	Name of Prospect					
	584	Name of Prospect					Prospects
	583	Name of Prospect					
	569	Name of Prospect					
	582	Name of Prospect					
	568	Name of Prospect					
	567	Name of Prospect					
	566	Name of Prospect					
	565	Name of Prospect					
	564	Name of Prospect					

Appendix B.

InterTech Customer Interview

Guideline

Section 0

This is the basic information you should have on a customer. You can use the customer interview to verify what you have or to get missing data.

Section A

These are general "warm-up" questions to get the dialogue going in a relaxed way.

Section B

The focus here is on customer satisfaction (value propositions) and loyalty indicators.

Section C

The first question elicits important satisfaction scores on your core products. But it also identifies cross-selling opportunities. You will find out some customers are not even aware of some of your products and services.

The questions then narrow down to budgets next year, competition, and share of customer factors. You will be amazed how responsive some of your customers will be to these questions. If they refuse to answer, do not protest; move on. (A refusal to answer a question is also important information.)

Section D

These questions give you an idea how often the customer wants to see you and via which media. You may also find people in the decision loop whom you did not know about.

Section E

These wrap-up questions can generate a lot of discussion . . . some orders . . . heretofore unspoken complaints . . . heretofore unspoken praise . . . or maybe just a firm handshake.

InterTech Customer Interview

Confidential

First of all, I would like to thank you for this opportunity. As I already mentioned over the phone, we would very much like to learn your views and identify your needs with regard to our technology and related products and services. Our first step is to ensure that our information on your company is up-to-date. Can we review it together?

---
0. COMPLETION OF CUSTOMER INFORMATION

Please complete this section as much in advance as possible; check it during conversation.

1. Customer mgr:...
2. Customer no: ....
3. Company name:...
4. Address:...
   ....
5. Postal Code:...
6. Town: ....
7. Country:..
8. Telephone no.:....................E-mail ....
9. Fax no.: ....

10. Division of: ....
11. Spoken to: ....
12a. DMU: ....
   ....
   ....
12b. Functions:..
13. Yearly Revenues:..
14. SIC Code:...

A. INTRODUCTION

A.1. What major developments have occurred in your company and line of business in the last 12 months?
....
....

A.2. Have there been any problems concerning switches and related components or technologies?
....
....

A.3. How could InterTech have contributed to solving these problems?
....
....

A.4. What kinds of requests, demands, or questions about electro/mechanical components are you hearing from your customers?
....
....

B. SATISFACTION MEASUREMENT

B.1. I am going to read you a list of aspects that you may look for in selecting a supplier of electro/mechanical components. Would you please tell me how you rate the importance of each of these items and your satisfaction with InterTech's performance with each aspect?
Importance: 5 = Essential; 4 = Very Important; 3 = Neutral; 2 = Not very important; 1 = Irrelevant
Satisfaction: 5 = Highly Satisfied; 4 = Satisfied; 3 = Neutral; 2 = Dissatisfied; 1 = Highly Dissatisfied

Product Characteristics and Quality	*Importance*	*Satisfaction*	*Comment*
1. Quality of construction	5 4 3 2 1	5 4 3 2 1	_____
2. Lifetime/durability/robustness	5 4 3 2 1	5 4 3 2 1	_____
3. Ease of Installation	5 4 3 2 1	5 4 3 2 1	_____
4. Range of Products	5 4 3 2 1	5 4 3 2 1	_____

Technical Service Quality	*Importance*	*Satisfaction*	*Comment*
5. Expertise of Technical Service	5 4 3 2 1	5 4 3 2 1	_____
6. Speed of Technical Service	5 4 3 2 1	5 4 3 2 1	_____
7. Delivery Times	5 4 3 2 1	5 4 3 2 1	_____

Relationship Aspects	*Importance*	*Satisfaction*	*Comment*
8. Understand our business and needs	5 4 3 2 1	5 4 3 2 1	_____
9. Offer useful ideas and suggestions (pro-active)	5 4 3 2 1	5 4 3 2 1	_____
10. Complaint handling	5 4 3 2 1	5 4 3 2 1	_____
11. Expertise of Account Manager	5 4 3 2 1	5 4 3 2 1	_____
12. Availability of Account Manager	5 4 3 2 1	5 4 3 2 1	_____
13. Do what is agreed before deadline	5 4 3 2 1	5 4 3 2 1	_____
14. Customer friendliness of contacts with you	5 4 3 2 1	5 4 3 2 1	_____

B.2. Are there any other items not mentioned that are important to you?

                          5 4 3 2 1   5 4 3 2 1   _____

                          5 4 3 2 1   5 4 3 2 1   _____

B.3 What are the most important reasons you have elected to do business with InterTech?

....

....

B.4. What specific suggestions for improvement do you have for InterTech?

....

....

B.5. To what degree do you or would you recommend InterTech to others?

❑ Definitely recommend ❑ Probably ❑ Neutral ❑ Probably not ❑ Definitely not

Comment: ....

....

B.6. In what supplier category do you place InterTech concerning our kind of products?

❑ Sole supplier ❑ Preferred supplier ❑ Equal with other(s) ❑ Secondary supplier ❑ Incidental supplier

Comment: ....

C. NEEDS INVENTORY

C.1. Let us now review your awareness and current use of InterTech products. We'd also like to know your level of satisfaction with the products you use.

Satisfaction: 5=Highly Satisfied; 4=Satisfied; 3=Neutral; 2=Dissatisfied; 1=Highly Dissatisfied

InterTech Product Categories	Aware	More info	Use	Satisfaction	Comment
Widgets	yes / no	❑	yes / no	5 4 3 2 1	_____
Plunkets	yes / no	❑	yes / no	5 4 3 2 1	_____
Johnson Bars	yes / no	❑	yes / no	5 4 3 2 1	_____
Whamos	yes / no	❑	yes / no	5 4 3 2 1	_____

C.2. Are there any plans or developments that might impact on your needs for these products in the next two or three years? ....

C.3. Taking a look at the shorter term, what do you estimate your budget to be for this year and the degree to which this is a change in the next 12 months?

Type of Product	This Year Budget	Expectations Next 12 months		
Widgets	....	Increase of ....%	Decrease of ......%	Stay about the same
Plunkets	....	Increase of ....%	Decrease of ......%	Stay about the same
Johnson Bars	....	Increase of ....%	Decrease of ......%	Stay about the same
Whamos	....	Increase of ....%	Decrease of ......%	Stay about the same

---

C.4. Do you meet your requirements with suppliers other than InterTech? May I ask which suppliers and your reason for choosing them?

Product Category	Suppliers	Reasons	% Budget
Widgets	....	....	....
Plunkets	....	....	....
Johnson Bars	....	....	....
Whamos	....	....	....

D. COMMUNICATIONS

D.1. In your opinion, how should InterTech keep in touch with you or your organization, and how often per year?

	Face-to-face	By mail	By telephone	Electronic (by e-mail)
General Manager	....	....	....	....
Account Manager	....	....	....	....
Product Manager	....	....	....	....

❑ Other ....

D.2. Would you consider ordering products from our Internet Web site?

❏ Definitely yes   ❏ Probably   ❏ Neutral   ❏ Probably not   ❏ Definitely not

D.3. Are there other persons involved in the decision process with regard to components, services, and other related technologies whom we should contact? And what role do they play in the buying process (buyer, user, decision maker, influencer)?

....

E. FINAL QUESTIONS

I would like to thank you for your contribution. The information you have given us is very useful. I have three closing questions:

E.1. Taking all aspects into consideration, to what degree are you satisfied with InterTech?

Satisfaction: 5=Highly Satisfied; 4=Satisfied; 3=Neutral; 2=Dissatisfied; 1=Highly Dissatisfied

E.2. Is there anything else that needs our attention at the moment?

....

E.3. Is there anything I can do for you personally? ....

Who   What   When

Thank you for your contribution!

Index

About the Authors

JAY CURRY was born and bred in Armonk, New York. He received a B.A. degree at Bates College and a Master of Science degree at the Boston University School of Public Communications. As an independent consultant specializing in introducing and implementing "direct marketing" in companies without experience in that discipline, Jay Curry was often confronted with top managers who had limited knowledge of direct marketing or were skeptical about its benefits. In 1989 he formulated the basic concept of Customer Marketing to resolve this problem. In 1991 he co-founded MSP Associates, an Amsterdam-based consulting company that helps larger and international companies implement CRM, using Customer Marketing as a platform. MSP Associates has served such clients as Xerox, DHL, Kimberly-Clark, ING Bank, Philips, and a number of other European companies.

Also in 1991, Curry completed the manuscript for his book on Customer Marketing, which was subsequently published in a number of editions in the Netherlands, England, France, Germany, Italy, and Brazil. His English-language books were published by Kogan-Page in London under the titles *Know Your Customers* and *Customer Marketing: How to Increase the Profitability of Your Customer Base.*

ADAM CURRY, the son of Jay Curry, was born in the United States and grew up in and around Amsterdam. As a teenager, he became enraptured with broadcasting and computers, the former based on his experience with communities ranging from citizen band to "pirate" radio stations, the latter stimulated by the early PCs and videotex terminals his father brought home in connection with the electronic publishing venture.

At the age of 19, Adam became a "veejay"on national television in the Netherlands, where he gained a wealth of experience presenting clips and interviewing top show business personalities. In 1987 MTV lured him to America, where he became a leading on-air personality for that fast-growing station.

In the late 1980s, Adam discovered the Internet, at that time still an academic network, and realized its potential as a revolutionary new medium for consumers and business. In 1994 he formed On Ramp, Inc., a company that had the mission to help major companies establish an Internet presence. He then melded On Ramp into a new company, Think New Ideas, Inc., which has become a leading interactive marketing communications company serving such clients as Budweiser, Avon, Gillette, IBM, Oracle, Procter & Gamble—even the Major League Baseball Players Association.